COOL SEASON
GARDENER

COOL SEASON
GARDENER

EXTEND THE
HARVEST,
PLAN AHEAD,
AND GROW
VEGETABLES
YEAR
ROUND

Bill Thorness

ILLUSTRATIONS BY
Susie Thorness

SKIPSTONE

Published by Skipstone, an imprint of The Mountaineers Books
Printed in the United States of America

First printing 2013
16 15 14 13   5 4 3 2 1

Copy Editors: Kris Fulsaas, Leighton Wingate
Design: Jane Jeszeck, www.jigsawseattle.com
Illustrations by Susie Thorness
All photographs by Bill Thorness unless otherwise noted.

ISBN (paperback): 978-1-59485-715-7
ISBN (ebook): 978-1-59485-716-4

Library of Congress Cataloging-in-Publication Data
Thorness, Bill, 1960-
Cool season gardener : extend the harvest, plan ahead, and grow vegetables year-round / Bill Thorness ;
illustrations by Susie Thorness. — 1st ed.
      p. cm.
Includes index.
ISBN 978-1-59485-715-7 (ppb)
1. Vegetable gardening—Northwest, Pacific. I. Title.
SB321.5.N58T46 2013
635—dc23
                  2012041688

Skipstone books may be purchased for corporate, educational, or other promotional sales.
For special discounts and information, contact our sales department at 800.553.4453 or
mbooks@mountaineersbooks.org.

Skipstone
1001 SW Klickitat Way
Suite 201
Seattle, Washington 98134
206.223.6303
www.skipstonebooks.org

5153 1548 4/13

LIVE LIFE. MAKE RIPPLES.

Contents

The seed is in the ground.
Now we may rest in hope while
darkness does its work.

—*Wendell Berry, "1991, V,"*
A Timbered Choir

Acknowledgments

This book did not germinate, sprout, and bloom from the efforts of just one gardener. First and foremost, it was made possible through the collective wisdom provided by many people over two decades of community and home gardening. Thanks go to all my garden mentors, both intentional educators and good old over-the-back-fence advisors. Among a large community of gardening friends, they are Julie Bryan, Sarah Cassidy, Carl Elliott, Arthur Lee Jacobson, Joanne Jewell, Josh Kirschenbaum, Rob Peterson, Howard Stenn, Ian Taylor, Lisa Taylor, and Carl Woestwin.

I'm also indebted to the books of Suzanne Ashworth, Linda Chalker-Scott, Binda Colebrook, Eliot Coleman, Rosalind Creasy, John Jeavons, William Head, and Steve Solomon; please see the Resources section for titles of their very useful books. The Miller Library at the University of Washington's Center for Urban Horticulture was invaluable, as was expert input from the instructors in the Master Gardener program operated by Washington State University/King County Extension.

Reviewers, sources, and consultants included Betty Barker, Doug Collins, Colleen Lochovich, Cliff Mass, Vern Nelson, Amy Ocherlander, Doug Oster, Kristy Ott-Borrelli, and Charley and Carol Yaw. My essential resource on anything having to do with building is journeyman carpenter and great friend Tim Olson. My first reader, cherished advisor, and wonderful illustrator is Susie Thorness. My expert editing collaborator, who always makes my work so much better, is Kris Fulsaas. I also am indebted to the excellent work and support of The Mountaineers Books and Skipstone staff and freelance contractors. Although these folks and others generously helped make this book better, I am solely responsible if it falls short of its goal or contains any incorrect information.

For my productive garden, and for the educational mulch that nourished this book, I offer heartfelt appreciation.

Introduction

Growing our own food is a delightful, productive pastime. Working with nature to cultivate edible plants from bare soil and a handful of seeds can be as nourishing to the spirit as it is to the body. The act of gardening, its many activities and chores, can strengthen and maintain a person's health. Of course, eating the fresh, organic food that we grow provides nutrition and much satisfaction.

So, if growing edibles is such a useful experience, why let it drop for three to six months each year? In some areas, the climate makes that choice for gardeners; it is just too cold for plants to grow, or the landscape is covered in snow. But in other areas, such as the maritime Northwest, the winter climate can be hospitable to the food gardener, and the garden can provide nourishment year-round. Why not try it?

To become a cool-season vegetable gardener requires a bit more planning and education, but under the right weather conditions, it is not a difficult task. It starts with the will to do it and a garden that gets good winter light. Add insulated gloves, a few specialized contraptions, targeted techniques, and some extra planning. Many people build or buy garden structures that extend the growing seasons by protecting plants from the harshest side of winter. They also employ proper timing and planting techniques, and take into consideration what grows well in a mild maritime climate. Because these tools and techniques are not given much attention in most gardening literature, this book attempts to tackle them in-depth.

Through a year-round lens, we'll look at the groundwork involved in gardening: enhancing your site and soil, understanding the weather, and getting your edible plants off to a good start. Then we will tackle those specialized cool-season methods and skills: expanding the growing calendar to seven mini-seasons, considering succession plans and maturity dates, and learning how to make and use many season-extending devices. The book also provides a listing of favorite cool-season vegetables, including suggested varieties, and a plethora of resources to help with the process.

Cool-season gardening actually begins in summer, when it's necessary to plan ahead and start

9

some fall and winter vegetables while the weather is warm. By late fall, the kitchen garden can produce a variety of delectable edibles. Expanding vegetable gardening to year-round production means you can serve up your own glorious green salad at Thanksgiving, robust beets at the winter solstice, fresh-picked leeks at New Year's, tender broccoli for Valentine's Day, and homegrown carrots on St. Patrick's Day.

A mild winter climate offers the chance to put garden-fresh food on your table—and feed your spirit by regularly communing with nature in your garden. And it's a way to get more productivity from your land. Growing food through all four seasons is like tripling the amount of space you have to garden.

But for me, gardening year-round means more than food *in* the garden, it also means I am growing *with* it. As I walk the paths daily, I learn from the seasons, lessons that radiate into other aspects of my life. Feeling the pace of the natural world teaches me patience or quickens my pulse. Watching and interacting with the web of life that exists from soil to sky provides perspective on my place in the system. Experiencing so much from my garden makes me want to just keep the cycle going, and growing, and growing ...

Part I
Laying the Groundwork

...es can be recycled into hot caps.

Lettuce starts in a plastic corral

...over the bed for a week or so before ...will warm and dry the soil. Once you ...nted, the cloche will allow you to regulate ...r on your seeds and tender seedlings. ...u start to fertilize, the cloche will protect ...ients from being washed away from plant

...u are a robust vegetable gardener, no doubt ...t seeds indoors. Moving the pots outdoors ...cold frame after the seeds have sprouted ...e the young plants more access to light and ...m ready for transplanting. Another alterna-...o start seeds outdoors under a cold frame. ...er your starts are in the ground or in pots, ...d frame provides even greater protection ...lustery spring weather. ...ating row cover—a finely spun fabric that ...s air, water, and some light through it—...d over garden beds also pays dividends in

spring. Adding a bit of warmth to the soil, this thin, permeable blanket encourages sprouting of whatever is in the bed, allowing you to skim off the unwanted plants and ready the soil for your vegetables. The protection helps the soil dry out a bit earlier than uncovered soil.

Enjoy the Pleasures of the First Sowing

Of course, spring sowing is the greatest joy of the season. I always anticipate the day when I can give my pea seeds a brief soak, dip them in inoculant, and line them up in a garden furrow. The curving necks of pea sprouts nodding their way out of the

Early spring in a Seattle P-Patch garden

Developing a
Seasonal Sensibility

An edible garden is all about the senses. Gaze over the lustrous sheen of ripe fruit. Feel the gentle resistance of the soil as you tug a root from the ground. Enjoy the fragrance as you brush by a bushy herb. Listen to the hushed rustle of cornstalks as they rub in the wind. And, of course, savor the sweet, crisp, tart, or earthy flavors of the homegrown bounty filling your plate.

These sensory experiences are at their height in spring and summer, but many gardeners are lured by those memories year-round. For instance, in winter I plan meals around my home-canned or -frozen produce, and a garden-grown dish spurs me to mull over what I'm going to plant in the spring or reminds me of brainstorms I had when working in the garden last summer that I want to put into effect next year. Because our garden senses are so tied to the seasons, this book begins with a look at how gardeners approach the traditional four seasons. In part 2, I examine how cool-season gardeners might expand their seasonal sensibility into seven miniseasons to satisfy those senses with fresh produce from the garden year-round.

SPRING

CELEBRATE SPROUTING!

Never does raw hope spring so nakedly from the pages of my garden journal as in spring. Exclamation points sprout up in my writing like garlic shoots pushing through straw mulch (although I resist a row of them, hoping they will appear to have naturalized into my garden prose rather than having been sown there; to continue the metaphor, I assiduously weed them out of most of my writing but make an exception for the exuberance of spring).

It's true that most gardens come alive in spring, but in a cool-season garden, spring comes early and settles in for a nice long stay. When gardeners in other climes are starting seeds indoors, a cool-season gardener who has planned ahead is out in the spring garden regularly, snipping leaves off overwintered greens and checking the size of broccoli sprouts and cabbages.

Regenerate with Early-Season Vegetables

It often does not take many weeks past the winter solstice for my mulched garden beds to begin showing signs of new life. In a mild winter with no

Viola tricolor

snow or freeze, the sprouting can begin as early as mid-January. First evidence comes from lengthening garlic shoots and new leaves on sturdier greens. When the garden has to recover from an icy spell, those signs could be delayed until early February.

Where I really begin to see signs of new life is under cover. If I have a cold frame, a cloche, or some other type of season-extending tool deployed over the soil, that protected ground is the first to come back to life. This is one of the most useful lessons of winter soil protection: the simple act of covering the ground with something—almost anything—helps the soil life remain more active, keeps the ground drier and more workable, and provides better conditions for seeds to sprout.

There's another lesson to be harvested from a covered bed: the weeds and wildflowers always come up first. In my garden, the Johnny jump-up (*Viola tricolor*), with its deep green, rounded leaves and cheery yellow-and-purple flower petals, can be found in almost any bed left fallow for a time. In some cases, if the crop rotation timing

Keep growing year-round with a cold frame.

is right (after harvesting broccoli in midspring, for instance), "weeds" like this can act as a cover crop and ably stand sentinel over the soil until I am again ready to use it. Sometimes I'm so grateful to such a helpful weed, especially one as pretty as this, that I hesitate to pull it up when doing my planting, often letting it stand around the edges of the bed. Being a little forgiving in this respect is a step that pays off, because I'm leaving some plants that eventually will go to seed again and sow the next cover crop for me.

Many times, too, the first seedlings to pop up under a covered bed will be shotweed (*Cardamine oligasperma*), which I run out of town on a rail

like an Old West sheriff, or tufts of annual grass blown in on a breeze or walked in on a waffle sole. I don't curse my shoes or the wind for that, though, because the breeze that carries the weed also carries my naturalizing garden seeds, such as arugula and corn salad.

One of the greatest pleasures of early-spring gardening under those covers is pondering the shapes of the tiniest sprouting leaves and, when they are large enough to determine where they fall on the desirability index, routing out the bad ones and thinning the good ones. If through a happy accident I get an entire bed of Asian mustards or a particularly prolific lettuce, I am in the enviable position of simply spacing out the starts widely enough to allow for their size at full maturity. Many times these tiny plants are so hardy that, if I pull them carefully from the crowd, they can be transplanted into other areas to fill out the bed.

For the cool-season gardener, spring can be the most fruitful time. All the effort that began the previous summer and continued into fall will show up on your table:

Plastic bo[...]

A varied bed of radicchio in a Por[...]

- The precocious growth spurts of overwintered plants has them leafing, budding, and flowering well before summer gardeners have even purchased their first vegetable starts.
- Root crops that have snuggled under mulch will brighten up with new leaf growth, and you will wait eagerly for the day when you can pull the carrots that have been sweetened by winter's chill.
- Plants harvested throughout winter, such as kale and collards, may begin to bolt when it is time to scoop them up for one big final feast.
- Stellar producers such as chard will amaze you with leaves so large they could be used to fan Cleopatra.

You will soon realize that yo[...] from your spring garden reg[...] including daily trips into the [...] pens before you have even dr[...] into the soil.

Amend the Environment

The cool-season gardener can [...] tools to get the spring season o[...]

Even if you are too busy dur[...] to pull out your large cloche for [...] spring is the time to dust it off a[...]

Placing [...]
planting [...]
have pl[...]
the wat[...]
When [...]
the nut[...]
roots.
If y[...]
you st[...]
under [...]
may g[...]
get th[...]
tive is [...]
Whet [...]
the c[...]
from [...]
F[...]
allow[...]
spre[...]

Garlic grows in a steel raised bed softened with rubber edges.

as cool as 40°F, and mustards, broccoli raab, endive, and Asian greens will not be far behind.

Two or three weeks further along, as you begin to snip crisp leaves off the first sowing of greens, Swiss chard and spinach can be sown. Then comes other early root crops such as turnips and potatoes, even carrots, going in about the time you are enjoying the first spicy bites of radishes.

By midspring, you will be turning your attention to the propagation and transplanting of summer vegetables, activities fueled by meals of the tender vegetables that you have been cultivating since early spring.

SUMMER

THINK AHEAD TO WINTER

At long last, warm summer days cause the tomatoes to ripen, so why would vegetable gardeners want to turn their thoughts to winter? Here's why: if you garden in a forgiving winter climate, what you plant during the warm days of summer can become a fall and winter bounty and help you get a jump on next year's crops. Plant in mid- to late summer, and you can have produce from your garden throughout the winter.

Two types of crops give many food gardeners autumn success in a mild climate: a second sowing of quick-growing veggies such as peas, radishes, and greens that will be harvested in late fall, and "overwintering" biennials (root vegetables, brassicas, even some onions) to provide a start to next year's bounty.

Cultivate a Different Perspective

Heat and lack of rain are elements that challenge summer sowing. It's difficult to keep a bed with good drainage wet enough during hot summer days to allow time for vegetable seeds to germinate

ground is a sure sign that another growing season has arrived.

If you use season-extending techniques (covered in chapters 7 and 8), the sheer variety of plants you can start earlier in the spring is impressive. These techniques can result in a banquet of spring veggies that will carry you into summer. With the lengthening days, it can seem almost possible to daily add a new vegetable to the mix.

Besides peas, my earliest starts include fava beans (which seem to sprout under nearly any conditions), radishes, and leafy salad greens. Lettuce and arugula will slowly emerge in soil conditions

This raised bed table provides waist-high gardening with shade planting below.

(although it doesn't seem to slow down the weed seeds much). Also, the soil in a bed that's just been harvested may be depleted of its nutrients.

Choosing a good place for your winter garden is important. When first trying cool-season gardening, you just plop your fall and winter seeds into whatever space happens to be open. With some planning, however, you can be more intentional next year.

Consider what your winter garden needs. Siting it in a warm, protected spot is ideal. Take into account wind protection as well as the amount of light that you will get from the lower angle of the fall and winter sun. Chapter 3 covers these topics in detail.

A raised bed, while a great technique to add drainage and maintain soil structure in a vegetable garden, presents a challenge to starting your winter garden. Because the bed drains faster and is heated by the sun (especially noticeable if the bed is made of stone), it may need more water to get the young shoots going. But those drainage and heat qualities will later aid growth in winter; chapter 7 describes this and the following techniques.

It is vital to give the winter garden a good start. Adding temporary shade helps the new seeds stay moist enough to germinate and keeps the young seedlings from wilting on a very hot day. Erect a cloche frame over the bed, and attach shade cloth or floating row cover material to it.

Light watering of a summer seedbed is generally a daily chore. Use a hose attachment that has a misting or very soft spray setting, or use overhead misters, rather than ground-level drip on your irrigation system.

A good way to hold in some of that water is to add compost to your soil. Top-dress the soil with a thin layer of compost and then plant into that. Or, if you're going to broadcast the seed across an entire bed, mix the seed directly with a small amount of compost, then sprinkle the mixture on the bed. Take care not to get the seed too deep under a mulch layer, or germination rates will suffer.

Plant Seeds or Starts?

Starting from seed provides the best choice in varieties, and some root crops must be sown as seed. However, many local nurseries carry a small variety of winter vegetable starts, allowing you to begin later and skip the seed stage for some crops. Chapter 5 discusses seed-starting and techniques to give your seedlings a good beginning.

Many vegetables have specific varieties that are better suited to a fall or winter crop and other varieties that will overwinter and provide a crop next spring. A lettuce suited to spring planting, for instance, may bolt or quickly go to seed if planted in warm summer weather. Therefore, it's important to review the recommendations for each variety that interests you. Chapter 9 contains information on varieties of cool-season vegetables.

Plan for Later Harvests

Choose varieties of greens that have a thirty- to forty-five-day period to maturity, so you can make salads from a summer planting by early fall. Continual sowing into late summer spreads out the maturity dates and provides salad until the first hard frost. In a mild fall, greens could grow until weeks after the last frost date. As autumn begins, swapping out the shade cloth for a plastic cloche cover can further extend the season.

Getting a good start on growth is the key for overwintering vegetables. If carrots, beets, or broccoli plants are a few inches high by winter, they can withstand most weather adversity.

While there is pleasure in creating a year-round vegetable garden, it's often difficult to get the timing right during summer vacation season. If you don't get it planted on time, don't despair. The next season will provide another, if different, angle on cool-season gardening.

FALL

SLOW DOWN AND PUT SOME GARDEN TO BED

It is said that a garden bench never rests its owner, but a nice fall day is the ideal time to sit for a few minutes and consider your vegetable garden. Besides being relaxing, this provides you with a chance to review the successes and failures of the growing year. You'll probably also notice some fall chores that need to be done and get you up off the bench, fulfilling the prophecy. At the very least, evaluate, take note, and plan for next year.

Take Time to Observe

Late fall is a good time to take a look at which varieties produced well, which didn't, why, and what you might do differently next year.

"Greens did wonderfully this year. I had a great crop of kale and chard," recalls Charmaine Slaven, a musician and Montanan who discussed year-round gardening with me shortly after she'd transplanted herself into Seattle's unique cool-season climate. "Also, this was the first year I successfully grew carrots." The desirable variety was Nantes, purchased from Oregon's Territorial Seeds.

Charmaine, who earns her seed money with the acoustic musical groups Tallboys and Squirrel Butter, "got into it seriously," gardening in both her front and back yards, keeping chickens, and taking classes. Her observations on light, water, and soil quality caused her to plan some changes. "My beets that got too much shade didn't do too well," she says, "so I'm going to try to clear some of the tree branches to let in more light. And I'm building the soil in the front yard."

Fall is the time for soil building, as cover crops can be sown into beds now cleared of their summer produce. Chapter 4 provides details on your soil.

Jot in Your Journal

Making notes on the cultural needs of your plants and this year's weather pattern will also help you next season. I keep a simple garden journal that includes planting dates, varieties, and soil amendments used. It also helps to record growing conditions, such as weather and rainfall amounts, because these have a great effect on the quality and quantity of the harvest. (For instance, in some years, the sad reality of a cool-season climate is too little summer sun to ripen all the tomatoes.) Finally, keep track of harvests and yield:

- What was that wonderful bean that did so well? Save seed or mark the catalog for next year.
- Did a winter squash or pepper put out small or too few fruit? If so, shop for a different variety, one bred for more vigor in our climate.

It's also useful to record which vegetables were planted where, so that you can practice effective

---

Gardening with Friends

Why keep all the joy of growing to yourself? Getting together with friends to garden is a great way to learn, share, and build community.

- **Share seeds.** Host a seed-sharing and -buying party in midwinter so people can find out what worked for others, share favorite varieties, and get new seed to use up while it's still fresh. Place one order, to reduce shipping cost and the carbon footprint of bringing those seeds to your door.
- **Share equipment.** We all probably have some garden tools or devices that we use only seasonally and otherwise store in the shed.

Create a sharing list and trade back and forth. It will save everyone money and the waste of duplicating tool needs.

- **Garden together.** Many people have more garden space than they can use, while others don't have enough. "Garden share" programs can turn a problem into a benefit.
- **Hold a "Weed and Feed."** Spring gardening chores can be daunting, especially if you've let things get a bit wild. But five or six people can whip a neglected yard into shape in one energetic afternoon, refueled by a communal meal. Schedule a series of free days with friends and move from yard to yard.

Garlic shoots mulched with leaves

crop rotation. Because of nutrient needs and the possibility of soil-borne diseases or pests, it is advisable not to plant the same veggies in the same place year after year. Chapter 4 discusses rotating crops, such as from a leafy plant to a root vegetable to a flowering plant to a fruiting one. "I plan to move my crops one to two beds over from where they were last year," says my musician friend Charmaine, "which I hope will keep disease down to a minimum. I do everything organically, so I'm really conscious of that."

Tuck in the Beds

If you're growing root crops that will overwinter (stay in the ground until spring), consider blanketing their bed with a layer of straw or leaves for protection against cold, windy conditions. I always get the urge to do that when the blustery fall winds denude the trees, sending leaves swirling to the gutters and drifting up along the bedding plants. Surely we will have success if we mirror mother nature's yearly ritual of covering her roots with a loose, warming blanket.

What Has Your Garden Taught You Today?

A garden is never finished. Even if you plant a forest of trees, you will need to manage the understory, thin them as they grow, and remove the ones that fall. Nature keeps things moving. In an untouched natural landscape, the forces of nature (wind, rain, snow, temperature, wildlife, et cetera) create a cacophony of actions. Something new is always taking place and, even in a minuscule way, altering the environment. Over time those changes cascade into a mighty tree falling or a river changing course.

We should allow a bit of wildness in our designed and manicured gardens. In fact, it cannot be avoided. But further, the effects of nature on our gardens should be embraced, because there are lessons to be learned.

New gardeners often seem to be worried about "doing things right"—as if making a mistake will result in failing the test and not being allowed to graduate into the fraternity of true gardeners. To me, a gardener is anyone who plants a seed, pulls a weed, or trims the vegetation. Whether doing a lot or a little, a gardener is one who embraces and learns from nature, knowing that understanding nature's ways will enhance our human efforts.

Determining success is not only about weighing the volume of produce that comes out of your garden. It is also about whether the garden has surprised, delighted, or taught you something. What has your garden told you lately? That you were foolish to attempt growing that tropical variety? That you planted those seeds too late in the season? That you cannot go away for a long weekend in summer without having someone water your winter vegetable seedlings?

I think failure in the garden is not paying attention to those messages from nature. It is refusing to learn from them. It is acting as though you are in complete control. Everything that happens in the garden is a lesson, and learning is a successful endeavor in itself.

A leaf layer protects bare beds from compaction during winter rains, as well as from desiccating effects of wind and frost. The mulch moderates temperature change and softens the effect of a hard freeze. A pile of leaves around the stems of woody plants or along a border naturally provides insect habitat too. Mulch on the beds increases earthworm activity and provides a haven for ground beetles and other beneficial bugs your garden needs.

If you're not growing cover crops or cool-season vegetables in some areas, mulch those beds with leaves 3–6 inches deep. Alternatively, or in addition, cover the beds with large burlap coffee bags (available from coffee roasters) to protect the soil. Chapter 4 expands on these ideas.

Gather extra leaves and keep them in dry bags or compost bins to use next summer, when the quantity of green compost material is high but the carbonaceous part of the mixture is scarcer. Leaves also make a great winter bedding for the worm bin.

Still Time for (Some) Seeds

Does putting the garden to bed make sprouting season seem far away? It may be too late in the fall for veggies you yearn to sow, but cover-crop seeds (see chapter 4 for details), such as hardy fava beans, can yet be planted. They will sprout in weather that would have other seeds turning to mush. Garlic also can be planted quite close to the frost date; it will survive in a cool-season garden even if it doesn't send up shoots until late winter. Calm the urge to plant even further by tucking a few flower bulbs of crocuses, daffodils, or tulips around the edge of the garden for a bit of color to brighten the garden in early spring.

In snow, a hoop-house cloche can resemble an igloo.

WINTER

TAKE TIME TO REAP AND LEARN

If you have planned ahead and have a vibrant cool-season garden, fall and winter provide the opportunity to reap the fruits of your labor and include your own produce in holiday meals.

I love spending Thanksgiving morning cutting greens from the garden for a big salad and adding to the meal wherever possible, such as using our own garlic, parsley, and sage in the turkey stuffing. Supplement fresh items by popping open a jar of home-canned produce from the summer harvest and cooking your own winter squash as a side dish or dessert pie. You might even round out the meal with fresh root crops—beets, carrots, or parsnips— and other summer crops still in storage, such as potatoes. The more home produce I can add to my holiday table, the more thankful I feel.

During winter, when weather in my cool– season garden veers from weak sunshine and short days to regular cloud cover and rainstorms or even snow flurries, it seems as if I spend as much time standing at the window looking out at the garden as I do standing over the plants. Even on the darkest days, however, it is important to get out for a regular walking review, even a brief one,

to see how things are surviving.

A lap through the garden is especially important if you have plants under season extenders such as cloches and cold frames. Monitor those plants for water needs, and vent the devices if they're in danger of overheating on a rare day of warmth and sun.

Take Stock

In general, the cool weather seems to slow down time, and a winter garden is a little more forgiving of neglect. Less time spent outside gives a gardener more time to ponder and study. I like to revisit my garden journal, reviewing what worked best, as I make a list for the coming seed order.

Finally getting around to reading new gardening books gives me inspiration, and I get an educational refresher by going back to my favorite old books and guides to remind myself of best practices. Trying new techniques comes from winter study, too, and each year I find different, and often better, ways to tackle some garden task.

During this period of thinking and reading, I take notes and sketch out my upcoming garden. I try to choose plants that will provide variety on the table, and that often means exploring a new cultivar or even a yet-untried vegetable. My notes and sketches map out my plan for succession planting (covered in chapter 6), charting where and what I will sow this year to give an ongoing harvest and the best use of my garden beds. Revisiting my textbooks on soil fertility (discussed in chapter 4), I chart my compost and fertilizer needs for each bed and plan my plantings based on the relative nutrient needs of each crop.

Usually I find that winter races by. As the rains decrease, soil warms, and days become noticeably longer, watching the plants shoot up does your heart good. Enjoy that feeling along with a meal of sweet overwintered broccoli and carrots, snipped and pulled just as the spring veggies are going in.

COOL-SEASON KEYS TO A SEASONAL SENSIBILITY

- Plan for the growing cycle to continue year-round.
- Observe, take notes, strategize.
- Learn from efforts that didn't quite work.
- Moderate the effects of weather with season-extending devices.
- Garden with a community of friends.

2

Understanding Our Weather

Whether you are a novice sky watcher or a certified meteorological forecaster, you will agree that weather has a great deal to do with the success of your vegetable garden. If you're gardening year-round, it is even more important to know a bit more than the average fair-weather gardener and to understand how to use the weather to your best advantage.

Fall and winter weather is often considered a barrier a gardener must overcome, but the cool seasons provide some benefits over summer gardening:

- **It is less work:** Things grow more slowly, there are fewer chores, and there is certainly less watering—at least by us!
- **Pests are not so prevalent:** Cabbage loopers generally aren't active below 50°F, for instance. Slugs and snails are exceptions, as they can continue to survive inside season-extending devices, and their eggs can hatch on even a warm January day.
- **Some diseases are less prevalent:** In winter, diseases such as powdery mildew are less viable.

- **It gives you a good reason to get outside:** On a nice winter day both your mental and physical health will benefit from a trip to the garden.

To get as much benefit as possible from the cool-season weather, it is necessary to understand weather patterns and expected conditions. As you're no doubt aware, weather conditions are not one-forecast-fits-all affairs. The weather can be pretty drastically different from one locale to the next. Even within a small geographic area, the microclimate in one garden can make conditions much better than in a neighboring property. In fact, it can turn a nearly ignored garden into a productive site and do wonders for a gardener's reputation. But the real gold stars deserve to go to those of us who don't garden in an optimal microclimate and still manage to get stellar results.

Let's examine the weather of the maritime Northwest and the conditions that create more positive microclimates. Western Washington, western Oregon, and coastal British Columbia all have a similar climate that is in large part defined by the Pacific Ocean. Because the prevailing winds move eastward over the ocean, picking up moisture and acquiring its relatively mild surface temperatures, the ocean is responsible for our rainfall, wind, and cloud patterns, and it moderates our temperatures year-round. The mild weather and moisture are held in by mountain ranges separating our maritime region from interior land that sees much less moisture and more extreme temperatures. While our mild summer weather might cause teeth grinding by those aching for long, hot days, cool-season gardeners owe the ocean a fathoms-deep debt of thanks. In a greater sense, all maritime Northwest gardeners serve at the pleasure of King Neptune, because we also get our winter snowpack—and hence our supply of summer water—from it.

The rain pattern through most of our region is quite predictable. Rain often increases to a roar in early November but may fluctuate in December. It rains steadily in January and February, and March can be wild, but we begin to see rain taper off. That brings us to spring, our longest season, which often begins before the vernal equinox in March—the traditional marking of spring in most places—and continues well beyond the summer solstice in mid-June.

I contend that summer in the maritime Northwest does not really begin until July 15, when the nights become shirt-sleeve warm and the rains virtually disappear. For the next few months, we can go weeks without any measurable precipitation. Our rainfall is at its lowest during our warmest summer period, when our burgeoning vegetable plot needs it most, ironically forcing residents of the maritime Northwest—living in a region with a reputation for being all wet—to water our gardens regularly. We start to see rainfall again in late September or certainly by mid-October, and our wet winter cycle begins again.

The coastal region from Vancouver Island to southern Oregon largely fits that pattern, although there are a few anomalous situations. The "Fraser gap" created by the Fraser River valley east of Vancouver, British Columbia, creates a trough that can bring cold air and winds from the interior down toward Bellingham, Washington, in the winter. A similar effect is caused by the Columbia Gorge, as fierce winds can swoop westward toward Portland, Oregon, and cause nasty ice storms and bitter weather. Unusual weather pockets exist on Washington's Olympic Peninsula and in southern Oregon, too. Sequim, on the Washington side of the Strait of Juan de Fuca, is in the rain shadow of the Olympic Mountains and thus very dry compared to its surrounding region, and that effect extends somewhat into Washington's San Juan Islands. The Olympic Peninsula towns of Aberdeen and Forks can get doused with extreme amounts of rainfall, while the coastal Oregon town of Brookings can get balmy in winter. Medford, Oregon, is unusually dry, too, being nearly surrounded by mountains.

ZONING OUT

You won't see details of rainfall patterns in the climate-zone maps put out for horticulturists by various organizations, such as the US Department of Agriculture or Sunset Publishing Company. But these zones can be useful for a "macro" look at your climate, especially if you're purchasing trees, shrubs, or perennials or considering moving to a new location.

The USDA Plant Hardiness Zone Map is based on the average annual minimum temperature in a location, with each zone divided into segments of 10°F. A long-awaited 2012 revision to the map used many more data points for the calculations and a longer data-collection period. That resulted in the addition of two zones and the shifting of many zone boundaries. The thirteen USDA zones are generally the ones referred to on plant tags. Although it's interesting to a vegetable gardener to know what the minimum temperature generally is in your area, that information is far from all that's needed to plan a year-round garden.

 Sunset Publishing has developed a much more sophisticated system based on "a broad range of factors, such as cold, heat, humidity, wind, proximity to the Pacific Ocean, snow cover, and the length of the growing season," according to its 2012 *Sunset Western Garden Book*. It breaks down the continental western United States, through the Rocky Mountain states, into twenty-four zones, plus two for Hawaii.

 Knowing your garden zone is useful when consulting Sunset's excellent reference book and when considering your landscape as a whole. Learning about expected conditions in your zone helps you make your garden into a thriving, diverse ecosystem. But zones are not as essential

---

What Will Global Warming Do to Our Gardening?

The well-documented effect on our planet of anthropogenic global warming, now usually called climate change, certainly should be a concern to gardeners. Many weather scientists predict that human-induced contributions to climate change will have disastrous effects and warn that we must take drastic actions to prevent extreme weather conditions, widespread drought, and inundation of coastal areas by rising sea levels, to name just a few expected results. By now, this is not a new message to most of us, and anyone who cares about the health and welfare of future generations, not to mention all the other species of life, will couple action along with that awareness.

 But does climate change mean that we will have to change our gardening practices? Not in the short term in the maritime Northwest, says climatologist Cliff Mass, professor of atmospheric sciences at the University of Washington in Seattle and author of *The Weather of the Pacific Northwest*.

 "Global warming is relatively slow around here because of the Pacific Ocean," he explains. "It really hasn't warmed up in the last twenty years. In fact, the Pacific Ocean has cooled off." Since we owe our weather patterns to the deep blue sea that licks the West Coast, we are spared some of the trends—for now.

 "There should be plenty of water" for maritime gardeners for the foreseeable future, he says, but that will slowly change. "The biggest issue will be the lack of snowpack, five to seven decades out." Mountain snow is where we get the municipal water supplies that we use to water the garden in our dry summers.

 Eventually—and this is good news for tomato growers—he predicts that "it will get warmer" in the region. "The growing season is going to improve. If you're a young person, it looks good for the gardening season."

 My take on it is this: Maritime Northwest gardeners can simultaneously act globally and locally to fight climate change. By growing our own food in our less-affected region, we can make a tiny dent in the greenhouse gases generated to grow, process, and transport food from other areas. And that should make the vegetables taste even sweeter.

for planting and tending most edibles (some perennial vegetables and herbs being exceptions). Other metrics are more immediately meaningful, and you will get more help by knowing how to read the local weather patterns and the particulars of your own landscape.

MICRO-STUDYING YOUR CLIMATE

Of primary importance is your own microclimate. Weather guru Cliff Mass, atmospheric sciences professor at the University of Washington in Seattle, defines climate in his book *The Weather of the Pacific Northwest* as "the average or typical weather of a location or region." I see a microclimate, then, as the average or typical weather of a specific location. Unfortunately, no weather expert can tell you exactly what it will be like this afternoon in your garden, although you can get a general regional forecast for the week ahead. To get hyperlocal, you must become a citizen meteorologist, which is exactly what Cliff advises.

"There are all kinds of wonderful ways to tell what's happening now that we didn't have twenty years ago," Cliff told me as I researched this book. Set out a rain gauge, "get a digital thermometer, and just walk around your yard and see what the temperatures are like." If you want to get serious and set up a home weather station, he suggests Davis Vantage Pro equipment. Another excellent step to take is to chart the prevailing winds on your site, making note of direction and strength at different times of the year. Jasmine-scented summer breezes might make your foliage feel fine, but winter gales can be very hard on your plants, due to extreme temperature changes and dessication of the plant's moisture. Wind protection is covered under site selection in chapter 3.

Many factors that influence your microclimate are important, Cliff says. "Proximity to water is a huge one around here. It's much warmer near water during the winter. Also, local topography; it makes a huge difference if you're in a valley or on a ridgeline. You can experience cooling of 5 to 10 degrees just by going down in a valley." On this, the professor had a very localized example: his own Seattle garden. "I'm in a valley, and I know exactly where the cold air is in my yard." He uses that knowledge as a gardener, which he says is mostly a summer pastime for him.

If you live in an urban area like Seattle, you may have cold spots in your yard, but you have an advantage over rural gardeners, because you dwell on a "heat island." In her book *Sustainable Landscapes and Gardens,* Linda Chalker-Scott describes the benefits and drawbacks of this phenomenon quite succinctly:

> *Urban areas experience what's termed the "heat island" effect, which means that temperatures in urban areas are always warmer than those in surrounding rural areas. This means urban dwellers can often push the envelope and grow marginally hardy plants successfully, but it also means that urban landscapes experience higher levels of soil water evaporation, leaf transpiration, and plant respiration (which uses energy reserves)—all of which can contribute to depressed plant growth. Surfaces such as asphalt that absorb sunlight and release heat further exacerbate that problem.*

Weather-Information Sources

Whether or not you can identify your microclimate, it is useful to get data from other sources, both local and regional. Even if you don't operate a home weather station, someone nearby may. Many people now have home weather stations, and some, like my neighbor Bob, put a station on their roof and a live link to it on their website. I can surf over there any time to see the temperature, wind speed, and rainfall record—right across the street. Bob's site even shows the temperature inside his house. That inspired me to put temperature and humidity sensors of my own inside my season-extending devices. I move the sensor from cold frame to cloche and can monitor air temperature to see when I need to get out there and open a vent. Cliff cautions that your neighbor's property may not be exactly like your own, though. "Take a few observations for a day or two," he says, and then compare it with your own data. "It may be close, but not close enough."

Many other online sources gather weather data. The city of Seattle funds Seattle RainWatch (www.atmos.washington.edu/SPU/), operated through Mass's UW department, which uses radar reflectivities and a rain-gauge network to display rainfall accumulation for the past forty-eight hours, along with a rainfall forecast. Seattle television station KING 5 (www.king5.com/weather) operates a regional network of schools with weather stations to feed their broadcasts. A Washington agricultural weather network, operated by Washington State University (www.weather.wsu .edu), provides air and soil temperatures, as well as many other variables, in real time for stations across the state.

In Portland, the *Oregonian* newspaper's Oregon Live website (www.oregonlive.com) aggregates weather from several sources and posts a daily weather blog forecast. A US Department of Interior site called AgriMet (www.usbr.gov/pn /agrimet/) offers in-depth weather details on many agricultural areas throughout the Northwest. A handful of stations are in western Oregon, including Forest Grove, Corvallis, and Aurora, all south of Portland. Some of the AgriMet sites

offer growing degree days calculations and even soil temperatures, vital metrics for farmers and very useful for cool-season gardeners as well. Both are discussed later in this chapter. The Weather Network in Canada (www.weathernetwork.com) offers a detailed lawn and garden forecast by city.

You can get local weather statistics and forecasts by punching your ZIP code into many websites, such as ones operated by the National Weather Service (www.weather.gov) and cable television's Weather Channel (www.weather .com). One of the best web weather services is Weather Underground (www.wunderground .com), which delivers the details along with a Google Maps–powered Wundermap that shows the local weather stations used to collect the data. If you're fortunate to live very near one of those weather stations, it could be *your* Bob-the-neighbor.

Frosty the Forecaster

Although intimate knowledge of your microclimate is essential, and local weather conditions and historical weather data are helpful, many food gardeners look for external guides as they study when to sow or transplant and calculate when they might expect to harvest. Timing your crops takes significant effort (and is treated extensively in Tricks of Timing in chapter 6), and many gardeners have been taught to follow the first and last frost date recommendations on planting calendars and seed packets to help them tackle this task. Just like the zone maps, frost date recommendations must be reviewed with a bit of skepticism by the year-round cool-season gardener.

"Our cool but moderate springs seem to last well into June, and long drawn-out cool fall weather often starts in late August and remains into November," writes Carl Elliott in the seminal *Maritime Northwest Garden Guide* by Seattle Tilth. "This makes first and last frost dates unpredictable. Therefore, when planting out or sowing, it's more important to focus on soil temperature." Soil temperature is discussed later in this chapter, but first let's examine the use and relative significance of frost dates.

Frost dates are estimated using data from the federal government's National Climatic Data Center (cdo.ncdc.noaa.gov). Frost dates are probabilities, based on the temperature records for a given area over a thirty-year time period from 1951 to 1980. Frost dates are calculated in temperature ranges that would result in a minor freeze (32–29°F), moderate freeze (28–25°F), or severe freeze (24°F or below).

The science of frosts and freezes is fascinating. For cool-season gardening activities, we are concerned mostly with frost rather than freeze. What most people think of as frost is called *radiational* frost (or ground frost or hoar frost). It occurs through condensation of moisture when the ground cools faster than the air temperature and ground temperature drops quickly below the freezing level of 32°F, resulting in a thin white covering over the landscape. When a harder frost occurs with lower temperatures accompanied by a cold wind, it's known as *advection* frost, and this is the killing frost that turns tender green plants into slimy brown masses overnight. (Although that description only skims the surface of this topic like a morning dew, I encourage interested readers to delve deeply into this fascinating topic through references given in this book's Resources list.)

Using the historical temperature data for your location and some computing power, you can find out when, to a stated degree of probability, your location could experience frost. The website

Dave's Garden (www.davesgarden.com) does a particularly good job of clearly delivering this information in a grid. Results show when your site will be likely to reach 32°F in the spring and when temperatures will likely drop to 32°F in the fall. Dates are correlated to probability ranging from 10 percent to 90 percent. When I put in my ZIP code, the site informs me that "almost certainly, you *will* receive frost from November 13 through March 19" but also that "you are almost guaranteed that you *will not* get frost from April 25 through October 7." My last frost date in the spring is therefore April 25, and my first frost date in the fall is October 7.

Summer gardeners can make good use of these data. If a seed packet tells me to sow seeds two weeks before my last frost date, I will plant fourteen days before April 25, or April 11. If I'm planting a tomato that will take 110 days to maturity, I can count back 110 days from my last frost date to make sure I have enough growing time to let it mature, and that will theoretically give me my transplanting date. So I could safely ripen a 110-day tomato if I transplant it by June 21—a fair bet . . . assuming I don't have a partly shady garden in a cool microclimate or that cool fall weather starts in late August, as my friend and former Seattle Tilth educator Carl Elliott observed. Former Washington State University Extension educator Holly Kennell advises that a gardener might add as much as 25 percent to the "days to maturity" calculation if the person lives in a cooler microclimate. So it seems that, again, weather data might be only as good as the hyperlocal conditions. If Bob's weather station had thirty years of daily temperature statistics, I could be virtually guaranteed that my calculations would be accurate.

USING A BETTER CALCULATION: GROWING DEGREE DAYS

There's another calculation that can be done with temperature data, and I think it's more useful to maritime Northwest gardeners, especially those who want to grow food year-round. It's called *growing degree days* (GDD), and it is found, like most things, through a handy-dandy website, in this case a multi-agency program called the Western Regional Climate Center (www.wrcc.dri.edu), hosted by the Desert Research Institute in Reno, Nevada.

Plants grow somewhat in response to the amount of heat they accumulate above a base temperature. (Other factors, such as irregular watering, affect growth rates, too.) Tomatoes, according to published research data, begin to grow at temperatures above 51°F. Their rate of growth increases proportionally to the temperature, depending upon how many GDD units, also known as heat units, the plants receive.

GDD is a calculation of the average daily temperature at a location minus the plant's base temperature—the lowest temperature at which it will actively grow. (Base temperatures are listed in the Cool-Season Crops chart in chapter 9.) The average daily temperature is calculated by adding a day's high and low temperatures (for example, a high of 80°F plus a low of 58°F on a nice summer day, equaling 138), then dividing by two to get the average (in this case, 69). Subtract the base temperature of a plant (let's say it's 50) and what you have left is the GDD (19). The equation would be 80 + 58 = 138, ÷ 2 = 69, – 50 = 19. So the GDD for that day would be 19. In many maritime Northwest places, the combined day and night temperatures don't reach lofty enough heights to generate any GDDs until well after the summer solstice. It's already summer in many places long before our degree days have begun.

GDDs accumulate over time, and even though they're measured in "days," they number well beyond 365 for a year. In the maritime Northwest, GDD units mostly accumulate from June through September. The most useful calculation is to come up with the total degree days you get in your garden in a year. That could be a more accurate "days to maturity" calculation for our region. Aside from finding GDD statistics about small grains that would be useful to farmers, however, I've never seen a chart that shows how many GDDs are needed to grow individual crops (wouldn't that be nice?). But I think your estimated GDD number can still be valuable. The relative number of GDDs at our location can tell us whether we can effectively grow long-season crops, or whether we should stick to the shorter-season varieties.

For instance, I can use GDD to compare my growing conditions to those of other places in the maritime Northwest and to those of places with truly warm summers. I can converse with fellow gardeners and find out what they can typically grow that I can't, thus beginning to gauge what my level of GDDs will allow. True science geeks could take this a step further by recording their actual temperatures each year and comparing those with the success of various crops planted at different times. After a few years, you'd have enough data to say which varieties are reliable and which are not worth the effort.

You also might begin to calculate more accurately the date you should start planting based on when degree days begin to accumulate at different temperatures. For instance, since lettuce begins growing at a base temperature of 40°F (rather than the 51°F of tomatoes), you could calculate at what date you'd expect degree days to begin with a base temperature of 40°F.

Boost Your GDD

The most valuable lesson from calculating growing degree days, however, comes from the use of season extension. By using season-extending techniques (discussed in chapters 7 and 8), you can artificially increase your growing degree days by a significant number. For instance, let's say you use a hoop-house cloche (covered in chapter 8) to start your tomatoes. In your location, you've calculated that you won't see much accumulation of degree days until late June. But in April you start measuring high and low temperatures in a raised bed with a cloche on it, and by May 1 you have nighttime temperatures in the low 50s in the cloche, so you know you can now safely plant your tomatoes under that cloche. During May, daytime temperatures reach 82°F in the cloche and nighttime temperatures hover at 53°F. Outside, the average maximum temperatures rise to only 67°F, and the average minimum temperatures drop to 48°F. Growing degree days for the garden outside the cloche add up to 237 for the month, but with the extra heat inside it, you've more than doubled that number, to 525. You have effectively brought July weather to your tomatoes in May. That's one great way to lengthen your growing season, and it can be done most of the year with different crops.

Take Your Soil's Temperature: A Foolproof Test

Being a humanities major in college and an ink-stained scribe in the thirty-plus years since then, I never developed a deep or satisfying relationship with science—that is, until I got into gardening. All of a sudden I'm charting the weather, calculating degree days, and tweaking my microclimate. I'm sure my few but long-suffering science teachers would be amazed. One of the most satisfying bits of science that I engage in is tracking my soil temperature.

Soil temperature is a measurement that comes as a feature on sophisticated weather stations, but it can also be measured with simple thermometers made specifically for soil use and sold at nurseries. Soil thermometers have a large aluminum housing that stands up to soil contact and can be either the liquid-in-glass or the dial type. Simply plunge them into the soil to a depth of 2–3 inches, wait a few minutes, and take a reading. If you move it, wait and let it recalibrate.

I use a couple of thermometers—one inside the cloche or cold frame and one in the uncovered or mulched soil (and, in fact, one with a really long probe in my compost bin). It's fascinating to see the difference between bare soil and the soil under a season-extending device. This is valuable information to keep in your garden journal and track from season to season. It is especially useful in the spring, because it tells me when I can begin to plant seeds.

Although there's no chart on the growing degree days needed for vegetables, the temperature range on when their seeds sprout is quite well researched and shared. For instance, lettuce needs cool soil to germinate; it will sprout at 40°F but does best in 50°F–65°F soil. Its germination rate drops off at temperatures warmer than that. Tomatoes, however, need a warm soil of at least 60°F and sprout much better if the soil is 70°F–85°F. (Optimum

soil temperatures for each crop are also listed in the Cool-Season Crops table in chapter 9.)

Using soil temperature, I can see the seasons changing as the red liquid inches up the soil thermometer's scale. During winter, the soil temperature sits stubbornly at 40°F in my bare soil and just slightly above that in the soil under the cloche. In the cold frame, I might see another degree or two of difference. When our climate has thoroughly chilled out for a while, even our season-extending techniques cannot make much of a dent. But give my garden a couple of nice days, and the soil under the season-extension devices begins to stir. First, the dial nudges up during the day, only to fall back into its winter trough overnight. But then it falls less and less, and by mid-February, it's holding steady at 45°F, while my bare soil is still slumbering at 40°F. That's when I start shaking the lettuce seed packs in anticipation, because I know I can begin the annual cycle once again.

READING THE SKIES

At the other extreme from plunging your temperature probe into the soil is casting your eyes skyward, looking to the horizon, and trying to take a reading on the weather. Can you tell what Mother Nature holds by scanning the cloud bank at sunset? When I was growing up in North Dakota, we could see storms coming from a hundred miles away, huge thunderheads—sorry, Professor Mass, cumulonimbus cloud formations—stacking up along the flat prairie horizon. Out on the farm, we'd chant the old saying "Red sky at night, sailor's delight; red sky at morning, sailors take warning." I'm not sure why we were so concerned about sailors, although we did have plentiful wind if they could have figured a way to sail their boats along the dusty furrows in our

fields. In any case, we equated a blazing red sunset as a good sign for fair weather the next day. These days, I can usually see the weather coming from the west a few hours ahead of time, but it's useful only for planning an afternoon bike ride and not reliable for even next-day forecasting. A colorful sunset most often comes when there's a sky full of clouds, and that could easily mean a stormy day to follow, or they could all have blown through by morning.

And really, what good is a one-day—or even a three-day or five-day—forecast to a gardener? True, I enjoy gardening when it's not cold and rainy, and if I know a spring deluge is upon us, I won't get out there with seeds in hand. At least, I always vow that, but then I'm forced to put on the slicker and do it anyway, because we all know what comes after two days of rain in the maritime Northwest: Monday.

But what would be most useful, especially to a year-round gardener, is knowing how hard a winter is coming and when to expect a warming trend to take hold in the spring. My wish list also includes a heads-up (email blast or a simple Twitter post would be fine) when a cold snap will hit us unusually early, say early November, when my winter veggies have not quite acclimated themselves to the cooling trend, or before one of those freak snows in April after the spring veggies have finally taken hold. Is that too much to ask? Apparently it is, because I haven't yet found an app for that.

However, there is plenty of predictability about our weather, and the good news is that our weather patterns will continue on course for the foreseeable future. The main reason seems to be the jet stream. That's the high band of wind that comes at us off the ocean, bringing our winter weather. It gets its moisture from the ocean, and because the temperature in our Pacific waters is always around 45°F–50°F, we get mild winter temperatures and mostly rain rather than snow.

Meteorologists are constantly tracking the jet stream's eastward-flowing giant slalom, which looks like an Olympic skier attacking a course, and a shift in the jet stream can hand us the gold medal of a dry weekend. On the other hand, if the jet stream, which can undulate hundreds of miles north or south, is aimed at us, it can easily pick up a low-pressure storm system and dump plenty of rain on us. Its patterns seem to be largely predictable. Just like migrating birds, the jet stream often moves north in the summer, taking its rains with it, which is why our summers are surprisingly dry.

Reports about the jet stream, though, pretty much tell us about just the next storm on the horizon. To prognosticate any further into the future, our weather folks look to El Niño and its counterpart, La Niña. These are "the only tools we have right now that give us any forecast ahead more than a few weeks," says Cliff Mass in his book. He describes the effects of this Pacific-originating phenomenon:

During the late nineteenth century, scientists realized that there was a regular variation in the surface temperatures of the tropical Pacific. The warm temperature phase became known as El Niño (the little boy), named for the Christ child because this warming usually begins around Christmastime off the west coast of South America. The opposite phase is La Niña and is associated with colder than normal temperatures in the tropical Pacific.

The book goes on to explain that the effect on Northwest weather is considerable:

El Niño winters are associated with warmer than normal temperatures and somewhat drier than normal conditions. La Niña years generally bring wetter and slightly cooler than typical winter weather.

Cliff notes that the cycle of moving from El Niño to La Niña and back occurs every three to seven years, and there are anomalous years when neither condition is evident, which wits in his field dryly call La Nada ("the nothing"). More temperature and humidity sensors in the Pacific, he says, will make forecasting these changes even better in the coming years.

So we can reliably thank "the little boy" for a warmer, drier winter, which should be a boon for the cool-season gardener.

COOL-SEASON KEYS TO UNDERSTANDING THE WEATHER

- Summer in the maritime Northwest doesn't start until July 15.
- Understanding your microclimate is vital.
- Monitor and record weather conditions regularly.
- Look for ways to boost your growing degree days.
- Track your soil temperature.

3

Siting the Cool-Season Garden

Walk out to your garden on a warm winter day with a folding chair under one arm, coffee cup in hand. Where will you settle? You'll probably want a sunny spot or at least an area with heat reflected off structures. You'll want a view of your beds and definitely protection from the wind. You'll want a dry spot—a place where, even if it had rained recently, the water has drained away and your feet will not get wet or cold. Even on a nice winter day, moisture chills the air, especially if it is windy.

Not to anthropomorphize, but your winter food garden plants thrive on basically the same microclimate that you intuitively seek. They want to bask in the sun and reflected heat, not struggle to remain upright in the face of strong winds, and not get waterlogged by soaked soil or roots. I admit, they may not care about the view.

Enhance your winter garden with raised beds and season-extension materials that face south and west.

Making a Place for Wildlife in Your Garden

Does your property provide food and habitat solely for your family and pets? As part of a larger ecosystem, reflect on how hospitable your backyard is to other species. Consider "what you can do to provide life needs for wildlife," suggests Russell Link, district wildlife biologist for the Washington State Department of Fish and Wildlife (DFW) and author of three books on wildlife in the landscape, including *Living with Wildlife in the Pacific Northwest.* The basic elements of a backyard wildlife habitat, he says, are food, water, shelter, and space.

Vine maple in flower

To meet those needs, hang a bird feeder, install a birdbath, nail up a nesting box, or keep companion animals out of the wild underbrush along your property's edge. To get more involved, create a pond or leave up the "snag" trunk of a dead tree.

Supporting wildlife through plant choices is another element of his approach. Two Northwest native plants, vine maple (*Acer circinatum*) and Oregon grape (*Mahonia aquifolium*) are among his favorites.

"Vine maple fits into urban backyards nicely," he says. "It's a great draw for flying insects seeking nectar early, including our native bees, and the flowers quickly form seeds that are eaten by chipmunks and many different birds." The small tree with its multitrunk habit also provides a dash of orange and red fall color to the landscape.

The evergreen shrub Oregon grape also provides early, bright yellow flowers followed by attractive purple fruits. "Our mason bees and other native bees pollinate the Oregon grape at the same time as our cherries, pears, and other fruit trees are flowering," he says.

"So by having those close together and having mason bees, you can help assure your fruit trees get pollinated."

If providing "supplemental" food sources such as feeders instead of edible landscape plants, Russell advises gardeners to consider the "maintenance and monitoring" required. Because, he says, "you can set up situations that are actually detrimental to wildlife," such as spreading disease between birds or attracting unwanted critters. Similar problems can result from nonmaintained birdbaths or nesting boxes.

But don't despair if your habitat creation turns sour. Visit the DFW website's section on "Living with Wildlife" (http://wdfw.wa.gov /living/) and click on a photo of a bothersome animal to open up a list of tips on managing the problem. The nonprofit National Wildlife Federation provides further help. The agency and wildlife group have partnered in providing a "Backyard Wildlife Habitat" certification program, by which you can be rewarded with a yard plaque for your efforts.

Permeable windbreaks such as a hedge or slatted fence slow winds, while solid fences cause pooling of cold air.

Walking around your yard with a chair will tell you a lot about where to put your winter garden. If you're in a new home or just planning your first garden, it will help if you're out there a lot, letting your senses tell you about the yard. Where the winds come from, where the shade falls on a sunny day, where the rain runs and pools are all instructive things to know. Your landscape provides interesting signals about your microclimate. My friend Lisa Taylor, in her book *Your Farm in the City,* suggests observing where the weeds first appear as an indication of what soil is warming up more quickly in the spring. Similarly, the areas where dew or frost are most evident probably are the coldest spots in the garden, and the softest, muckiest ground in winter likely contains the soil with the worst drainage.

Wind protection, solar exposure, and good drainage are three key elements to selecting the best site to grow edibles in winter.

WIND PROTECTION

Even though the maritime Northwest enjoys a relatively mild winter, our cold season definitely comes with some harsh conditions for plants.

Chill winds and pounding rains are the two biggest culprits. Finding or creating a protected spot is the best defense and helps mitigate the effects of our winter weather.

The invisible power of wind should not be underestimated. It can drive rain sideways in the winter, bring in a killing frost, or thwart nature's pollination process. For those reasons, gardeners try to lessen the wind exposure to tender plants such as annual vegetables, especially ones grown in our cool seasons.

Permeability

Once you've tracked the prevailing wind direction during the cool seasons, see if you have the space to create a windbreak, a great technique to improve your microclimate. Windbreaks can be made of many things, but the one thing they should not be is a solid wall, such as a continuous wood fence. If you have a fence like this—in which each board is butted up against the next—go out one windy winter day and see what it's like next to the fence. It blocks the wind, but you won't find it very calm on the other side. Instead, a solid wall creates turbulence: the wind climbs vertically

Cold frame and cloche angled so their broad, sloped sides face the sunniest southern exposure

over the top of the fence and then swirls down in a clockwise motion on the leeward side of it. On the back side of a fence like this you'll often find a cold spot—possibly the coolest area in your garden. Your winter vegetable garden will not thrive right next to it, but it's possible to build the garden 8–10 feet away from the fence, far enough for those swirling eddies of wind to dissipate.

A permeable fence or a hedge handles the wind much better, because it slows it down but doesn't completely block it. This partial diversion makes your garden calmer and doesn't create conditions in which the wind pools. Instead, the wind will gradually return to its free wind speed the farther it gets away from the permeable barrier.

When you're first building a winter garden, a temporary windbreak is advisable because you can test its effectiveness and whether it casts shade on your garden. Once you've studied its effects, you can build or plant a permanent windbreak. These are some choices for windbreaks, both temporary and permanent:

- An evergreen hedge, using an edible, bird-attracting plant like our native evergreen huckleberry *(Vaccinium ovatum)*
- A wood fence with staggered slats that have space between them
- A deciduous hedge, perhaps a Belgian fence of espaliered small apple trees, with branching thick enough to create a noticeable reduction in wind volume even after the plants drop their leaves
- A combination of evergreen and deciduous plants (go Northwest native with a mix of vine

The flat sides of these raised beds help the soil become warmer and drier earlier in the season.

maple, evergreen huckleberry, and tall Oregon grape) to provide year-round landscaping interest as well as the permeable barrier you seek

- A temporary winter fence of bamboo poles, summer trellises not currently in use, pruned tree limbs lashed together, or recycled building materials
- A "compost fence," in which you build up compostable materials such as twigs and leaves between two wire-mesh fences set a few inches apart; the materials degrade and settle over time but, meanwhile, offer that vital protection

Height

When you add a structure or hedge to the garden, whether for a windbreak or other reasons, consider not only its permeability but its height. Just as there's a relationship between permeability and turbulence, there's a relationship between the structure's height and the distance beyond the structure at which the wind returns to its full speed. The taller your structure, the more space on the other side of it that will enjoy reduced wind speed, but also the farther the structure will cast a shadow. Be careful not to put any barriers between your winter vegetable garden and that shy yellow orb that sometimes peeks through our cloudy winter sky.

SOLAR EXPOSURE

It's vital to track the light exposure in your winter garden. Even though the solar gain may be minimal on cloudy days, there is always some light to be had. And when we do have a clear sky, or even when the clouds blow away for a time on a change-able afternoon, the warming sun boosts vegetable health as much as it benefits our spirits.

Our latitude in the maritime Northwest means gardeners always need to track the sun, even at the height of summer. In the other seasons, it skates along at a lower angle that can cast long shadows, making it even more important to study what will be in between it and your garden. Deciduous trees that shade your garden in summer might be no problem in the winter, but you'll need to site your garden far enough away from a line of evergreens or that protective hedge to avoid the shade. Track the sun at midday, but also make notes at other times, too, observing the following:

- What time of day does the sun hit your garden?
- When do afternoon shadows start creeping over the beds?
- How does the pattern change at different times of the year?

Here's a useful procedure for someone who's around the garden regularly, for instance, if you work at home or are a stay-at-home parent or retiree: check the sun and shadows at regular times of day, perhaps 9:00 AM, noon, and 3:00 PM. You could even take some garden stakes—bamboo or the bundled wooden construction stakes you can buy at a lumberyard—and mark the edge of the shade in your yard at noon on every sunny day for a couple of months. Such close observation is the best way to see what patterns emerge.

Reflective and Radiant Heat

Besides delivering the essential element for photosynthesis, sun exposure also provides other benefits to the cool-season garden: reflective and radiant heat.

Light-colored walls and structures reflect the sun's rays, adding reflected heat to the surrounding area. Radiant heat comes from the sun's warmth being absorbed by dark-colored objects such as soil; by dense, porous materials such as stone or wood made into raised beds; or by purposeful "heat sinks" such as jugs of water placed in the garden. Because those objects will be warmer than the surrounding air, the heat radiates from them to equalize the temperature. That happens relatively slowly and provides more warming effects on the landscape than direct sunlight alone. The dark soil of a garden bed warms up more than a green lawn, and flagstone pavers radiate more heat than a dirt path.

Put those concepts about sun exposure to work with proper site selection. Consider the surrounding hardscape, and site your winter garden to get the most possible reflected and radiant heat. A south-facing garden is best; west is second-best. The east and north sides of a property are almost always the coldest and darkest, because houses and garages shade those areas. Up against the south wall of the house might be best or on the middle level of a set of stone terraces.

Enhance these locations by creating more heat-absorbing and -reflecting structures, such as raised beds (discussed extensively in chapter 7). Some techniques used to gain more solar effect can also benefit another major consideration in site selection for a maritime winter garden: drainage.

RAIN MITIGATION

What do you do with all that water coming down to pound the soil all winter? It's the conundrum faced daily by a cool-season gardener, and as with any good challenge, there's no easy or direct answer. My strategy is a combination of good drainage, absorption, and deflection.

Drainage

The first part of the rain-mitigation plan comes into play during the site-selection process. Your garden soil could have any number of conditions that cause less-than-optimum drainage. If it's a new home, the contractor may have compacted the soil by driving heavy equipment on it or storing building materials on it for months. Uninformed contractors often follow up that procedure by rolling out a carpet of sod and calling it done, which just transfers the problem of compacted soil to the homeowner. But compaction might not be your problem at all—you just might have lousy soil. Maritime Northwest soils can run the gamut from heavy clay to light sand. Whatever soil conditions you inherit need to be addressed (more details are given in chapter 4).

Compacted or heavy clay soils often suffer from bad drainage. Other conditions, such as your site's being located at the bottom of a slope or adjacent to a great deal of nearby impervious hardscape, can also contribute to water saturation on your property that makes drainage problematic.

When siting your cool-season garden, you must know what drainage conditions exist. Once you've scoped out the best site from a sun-and-wind-exposure standpoint, try this test: Dig a hole at that location, 2 feet deep and 2 feet wide. Fill it up with water and let it drain out. Fill it up again. If the water does not drain out of the hole in a few hours, you have a drainage problem.

Test the drainage in all possible areas—you may be able to revise your garden location. But if you have bad drainage in your prime spot, paraphrase the old real estate slogan "You can change the bed, but you can't change the location," and don't despair. That's what raised beds and pervious paving are for! Raised beds are discussed extensively in chapter 7, but a couple of thoughts

A cement paver grid provides drainage, planting pockets, and a non-skid surface.

here on pervious pathways might be helpful to address water issues.

Absorption

The term *pervious* has come into common use in the landscaping world recently, and it's a good way to describe paving materials that help deal with water. I've seen pervious concrete sidewalks in a park, pervious asphalt used as a residential driveway, and all manner of pervious paving systems used for walkways. My favorite, although not the fanciest type, is an open grid of concrete that is great for sloped or flat paths and could be used for driveways. Each panel is 2 feet by 3 feet with a pattern of 6-inch diamond-shaped holes. The panels, set on a paver base material, can be fitted together for a continuous surface, and the holes can be filled with soil, into which you can plant mosses or other "steppable" plants. It's much less expensive than interlocking bricks or large slabs of quarried stone and has an organic look, as the gray concrete can almost disappear under the ground-cover plants. It also does a swell job of absorbing copious amounts of rain—which is the goal of a pervious system.

Having a pervious hardscape pathway to the vegetable garden is essential for gardening in the cool season. It makes it so much easier to visit the garden regularly, which we've already established is good for the spirit as well as the plants. Although the weather is not ideal, you need to get out there. Weeding and watering chores taper off in winter, but they don't disappear. And you'll be adding season-extending devices such as cloches and cold frames, which need to be vented on sunny afternoons. Even on a stormy day, you'll want to dash out to snip some lettuce or pull a parsnip. All these activities are so much nicer if you don't get your shoes covered in muck or tramp a path into a soggy lawn.

Deflection

My final defense against the maritime Northwest's copious winter rains is to deflect a lot of the rain away from the beds where I grow a cool-season garden. This is primarily done with season-extending cloches and cold frames, which shed the rain off their plastic or glass surfaces. Chapters 7 and 8 delve into the use of these devices.

A form of deflection is to grow a cover crop on any garden soil left bare in winter. Cover crops decrease the effect of winter rain. Nitrogen and other nutrients can leach from the soil into groundwater and wastefully drain away. Compaction from rain can reduce soil air space and break up the good soil structure needed for healthy plant roots. Cover crops help by shielding the soil from the hammering effects of rain, preventing or reducing compaction by sending their roots through the soil, and building soil structure in other ways, such as breaking up clay soil or binding up sandy soil for better water retention.

COOL-SEASON KEYS TO SITING YOUR GARDEN

- Choose a protected, accessible spot: sheltered, south facing, and on a slight slope for drainage.
- Add permeable wind protection, such as a hedge.
- Observe sun patterns: see what's in shadow at midday.
- Manage winter rain through drainage, absorption, and deflection.
- Establish clean, easy winter access.

4

Building the Soil

There is an intertwined pulse between the natural world and human lives, and I sense it every day of the year in my garden. It seems that nature is a creature of habit, just as habit is the nature of creatures. It is fascinating to watch and be a part of the cycle.

In spring, I get at eye level to glory in the pale green stems shooting from the musty crust of the earth like the hands on a clock rising to trigger a wake-up call. During summer, the course of the day starts with the call of robins outside my window at 4:00 AM as they sense the impending dawn. By autumn, winds are throwing a jigsaw puzzle of red and yellow and brown leaves into the air in front of me. Deep in a maritime Northwest winter, the plinking, pooling rain washes our celebrated storms right up to my doorstep. To each of these signals, and to many more—new ones virtually every day—I react. What I do, eat, wear, sing, read, dig, and plant is in response to all that input.

Sorting out the signals and making habit of the natural responses is what keeps my garden going all year-round. Those spring shoots need a fertile soil to get the best start. Summer robins are so annoyingly cheerful because their favorite food—the earthworm—is in plentiful supply. Kicking through autumn leaves reminds me to nurture my soil with its mulch blanket, and winter rains are less impactful (and compactful) on my soil if I've done my autumn mulching and cover-cropping chores.

Responding to the cues means looking after my soil, planning and planting an evolving selection of crops, building the garden ecosystem, mulching, cover-cropping—in short, a year-round menu with the word "tending" at the top, followed by a rotating list of tasks chalked in and checked off. For each of these steps, there is a season, and for some it's a continuous effort. It helps to have an awareness of this changing *carte du jour*. Let's tackle these in order of attention throughout the year.

TEST YOUR SOIL

The first key to a successful garden is to have healthy, fertile soil, and it is essential when growing plants in the more challenging environment of our cool seasons. You get to know your soil more deeply by doing a soil test.

Soil testing in the maritime Northwest is best done in fall. At that time, your summer vegetables will have finished their uptake of nutrients, and you'll be going into winter with a baseline level of the elements needed to grow edibles. A fall soil test gives you plenty of time to plan what you need to do to replenish the nutrients while you decide what to grow in the beds next spring, and it will tell you if you're leaving too much fertilizer in the soil after the main growing season. If you test more than once, testing at the same time of the year gives valuable comparison measures.

I do not get a soil test every year. It would be interesting to track it that closely, but why waste your or the lab's effort (or your money, if you have to pay for it) if you will see very little change from year to year? I think that in an established garden with good production, a test every few years to keep you on track should be all that's needed.

Year-round gardeners rotate another crop into the beds that get the soil test, and that can present a challenge. However, with lower light conditions and, thus, less photosynthesis, the slower rate of plant growth in the fall and winter means less nutrient uptake by plants. With your fall soil test in hand, it's a simple matter to correct deficiencies of nutrients that you know will be needed by your fall and winter crops.

My standard soil test comes free from the King Conservation District, which provides the service to residents of my county as a way to promote appropriate fertilizer use because excessive fertilizer can leach into groundwater and local waterways, causing problems. I've considered home soil tests but hear regularly from horticulturists that such tests can be pretty inaccurate, so I leave it to the lab. The simple litmus test for soil pH, readily available in an inexpensive kit at nurseries, is the exception, but even that should not be necessary if you get a professional soil test periodically and have good soil-fertilization practices.

A laboratory soil analysis can test for many things, the basics being primary and secondary nutrients, trace minerals, pH, and level of organic matter, which is the living part of the soil comprised of decomposed plant material (like compost) and the soil food web surrounding it. My lab also provides the soil's cation exchange capacity (discussed below). You can pay labs to perform more tests and offer other detailed results; check with your local university extension office for recommended labs. Seek an analysis that tests for heavy metals if you're gardening on land near an industrial area or even next to an old house whose paint may have contained lead. I tested for metals when starting my garden and now am content with tracking the basic information.

To perform the test, homeowners send some fresh core samples of their soil to the testing company. The agency provides instructions on how to take a soil sample and prepare it properly for submission. In my case, the results usually come back in a couple of weeks. Not only does the report tell me what nutrients are in the beds and the ability of my plants to take them up, but the lab also offers recommendations on how much and when to fertilize.

Last time I dug holes for the soil test, I sat on the edge of the raised bed and considered what I was holding, taking a minute to be amazed at what I can't see. A handful of soil is basically a brown clump or pile, maybe with some rocks, the occasional small critter, decomposing roots and twigs, and some flecks of things that glint in the light. One major benefit of a soil test is to get you thinking about what useful elements are attached to the sand, clay, and rocky mineral particles that make up your soil.

What Nutrients Are Down There?

Scientists categorize the fourteen soil elements needed by plants as primary nutrients, secondary nutrients, and micronutrients or trace minerals (see the Know Your N-P-K ... Plus 11 sidebar). A proper balance of nutrients not only feeds your plants but also keeps the soil food web of microscopic soil life busy and healthy, too.

Primary Nutrients: N-P-K

Primary nutrients are the ones needed in largest quantity by your plants—the nitrogen, phosphorus, and potassium (N-P-K) whose percentages are written in big letters on fertilizer labels.

Nitrogen, the "N" of the N-P-K equation, is primarily responsible for overall plant functions and promotes robust leaf growth. It is the most commonly depleted primary nutrient in our soil. It is also the most readily available because it is generated organically—through the application of compost, from the breakdown of plant materials, and by biological "fixation" of it by soil bacteria onto the roots of some plants.

If you add nitrogen in the spring and deplete it by fall, there is less to leach out into groundwater or wash into surface water when winter rains begin. However, if your soil test shows you have high levels in the fall, you're possibly fertilizing too heavily. At the very least, the test will show where you don't need to add nitrogen to grow your veggies. Nitrogen also can accumulate too heavily in winter plantings of some crops, so it helps to be aware of soil nitrogen levels to choose the best beds for those winter vegetables (see the Reducing Nitrates in Leafy Greens sidebar).

Phosphorus, the "P" of the N-P-K equation, promotes root growth and helps bring plants to maturity as they flower and produce seed. Too much can also damage water ecosystems, especially when it causes algae blooms or excessive growth of other aquatic plants. Phosphorus is released slowly to your plants and is not depleted as fast as nitrogen.

Potassium, the "K" (which stands for *kalium*, the element's Latin name) of the equation, supports overall plant growth, helping plants absorb other nutrients and effectively transport water. It is important for plants' disease resistance and tolerance of extreme conditions, so adequate levels are essential for cool-season growing.

Secondary Nutrients

The three secondary nutrients (calcium, magnesium, and sulfur), while needed by your plants and soil food web in smaller quantities, are equally as important as the primary N-P-K nutrients.

Calcium supports cell development and helps plants absorb nitrogen, which produces healthier plants with better disease resistance. It is the main ingredient in agricultural lime, which is used to "sweeten" the soil and bring the pH into a healthy range for vegetables.

Magnesium is the central part of the chlorophyll molecule. It helps seeds germinate and

Get a close-up view of the soil when planting seeds.

enables plant uptake of other elements. It is sometimes deficient in maritime Northwest soils. Many gardeners restore magnesium levels with an application of dolomitic lime.

Sulfur is a component of plant enzymes and proteins that also govern plant functions such as photosynthesis. It contributes to the flavor of some vegetables, such as onions, garlic, and broccoli. Sulfur may be leached out of the soil, but it is commonly available in compost, manure, and fertilizers, so it is rarely deficient in our soils.

Micronutrients

The eight trace minerals, or micronutrients—boron, zinc, copper, manganese, iron, molybdenum, chlorine, and nickel—although needed only in small quantities, play key roles in plant formation, from photosynthesis to hormone production to cell-wall development. Most are commonly available as trace minerals in soil and in organic fertilizers, so gardeners need not worry about adding extra amounts of them.

Of these eight, however, boron contributes to growth in some brassicas, and it can be leached out of maritime soils. Because many beloved cool-season crops come from that genus, winter gardeners might want to pay particular attention to boron levels in their soil tests.

Of course, there is much more to know about each of these trace minerals, and a delicate interplay is at work as they simultaneously feed the plants and soil life. Even if a home gardener doesn't study the science, though, you can maintain a healthy soil by following soil-test recommendations and using cover crops and compost to boost organic matter levels.

Know Your N-P-K ... Plus 11

These fourteen soil nutrients are elemental to plant growth.

Three primary nutrients:
- Nitrogen (N)
- Phosphorous (P)
- Potassium (K)

Three secondary nutrients:
- Calcium (Ca)
- Magnesium (Mg)
- Sulfur (S)

Eight micronutrients, or trace minerals:
- Boron (B)
- Zinc (Zn)
- Copper (Cu)
- Manganese (Mn)
- Iron (Fe)
- Molybdenum (Mo)
- Chlorine (Cl)
- Nickel (Ni)

What About pH and Nutrient Adsorption?

Two additional areas of a soil test can help determine whether your soil is effectively supporting plant growth and whether you need soil amendments: pH level and cation exchange capacity, which relates to nutrient adsorption.

Soil pH

The pH level tells you whether your soil is acidic, neutral, or alkaline. If the soil test shows a low pH number, your soil is acidic; if the pH number is high, your soil is alkaline. Vegetables grow best in the 6.0- to 7.5-pH range, and 7.0 is neutral pH. Acidic soils can be a problem in the maritime Northwest, primarily due to high rainfall and leaching of calcium and magnesium, which buffer the soil's pH. Thus, your soil test might also show a deficiency in calcium and magnesium levels. Your pH level can be adjusted by *liming the soil,* adding

Reducing Nitrates in Leafy Greens

A recent study of nitrates in winter-grown vegetables, in the form of nitrate-nitrogen (NO3-N), was conducted by Washington State University research associate Kristy Ott-Borrelli, in which she reviewed the body of previous scientific literature and performed two seasons of field testing. Her study showed significant accumulation of nitrates in leafy greens of lettuce, spinach, and Asian salad greens. The highest concentrations were found in Asian greens from the *Brassica* genus. Low winter light levels can cause more nitrate accumulation in plant cells, due to physiological activities in the plant and lower rates of photosynthesis.

Although science has not yet provided definitive answers, the nitrate levels detected could be harmful, causing some regulators to act. The United States does not have a regulation on acceptable levels of nitrate-nitrogen in vegetables for sale commercially, but the European Union has studied and set limits on it in leafy green crops for the EU's agricultural system.

Of primary concern is the ingestion of nitrates by infants, because it can cause acquired *methemoglobinemia* (blue-baby syndrome), a significant but treatable condition. Though it's unlikely that babies eat fresh garden greens, Ott-Borrelli advises parents not to feed their babies canned spinach or greens.

In adults, some studies suggest nitrate accumulation is a cancer risk, and other health problems have been studied for possible correlation. However, other recent studies have suggested that nitrates may help with cardiovascular health. With such muddied waters, I think it's best to do what we can to keep nitrogen levels in our winter vegetables low as we monitor ongoing research. Here are some ways to reduce high nitrate intake:

- Fertilize with compost or organic fish or kelp fertilizer. Plant uptake of nitrogen from these is slower than with chemical fertilizers.
- When picking and eating spinach, lettuce, and Asian salad greens, use only the leaf blades. Ott-Borrelli found much higher nitrate concentrations in the *petioles* (the base of the leaf where it connects to the stem) than in the leaf blades.
- With spinach, use only younger leaves. The research showed that nitrate concentration was higher in older, larger leaves on the outside whorls of spinach plants.
- Don't eat the center or "heart" of head lettuce. One study showed much higher nitrate concentrations there.
- Choose varieties with smooth or semi-savoyed (crinkled) leaves. Heavily savoyed varieties have higher nitrate concentrations.
- Pick leafy green vegetables in late afternoon, when tests have shown nitrate levels to be lowest.
- Eat leafy greens immediately after harvesting or store them with proper refrigeration. Nitrate levels rose as the vegetables aged in room-temperature conditions.

calcium in the form of ground limestone—or dolomitic lime if your soil test also shows low magnesium levels.

Soil pH is important beyond having proper amounts of those two elements, however. There is a correlation between the pH level and the availability of many soil nutrients. The nutrients become increasingly available as the pH nears the neutral range of 6.0 to 7.0 and then will drop off again if the pH lowers or rises out of that range.

The way that happens is fascinating, and it's the final leg in the scientific three-legged stool of soil fertility that I balance on when I read my soil test.

Nutrient Adsorption

Clay and humus particles have a negative electrical charge and can hold a certain level of positively charged nutrients. Elements with a positive charge are called *cations,* and the amount of cations the soil can hold is known as cation exchange capacity (CEC). This process of adding positively charged elements is called *adsorption,* which means the bonding of an element onto the surface of the soil particle, versus *absorption,* in which one substance is taken *into* another.

A proper pH level increases the adsorption quality of humus particles so they can grab more of the positively charged nutrients that are important for plant growth, such as potassium, calcium, and magnesium. With high organic matter levels comes a higher CEC, and more of these nutrients are available for the plants.

So how do I use the soil test to affect its CEC? It's useful to know that different soil types have different CEC levels. Organic matter has the highest capacity to make these cation exchanges, so if your soil has a high organic matter level and proper pH, you have created the best environment

for nutrients to get to your plants. Thus, you'll need to use less fertilizer.

FERTILIZE STRATEGICALLY

Year-round gardeners need to pay extra attention to fertilizer needs, especially because we are asking the soil to feed plants continually. I recommend rotating the winter crops (discussed later in this chapter) and regularly letting each garden bed rest. You also need to keep an eye on the pH, the level of organic matter, and the level of nutrients in the soil of every bed, which tells you when to add fertilizer. Consider both the type and timing of fertilizer.

What Type of Fertilizer?

I use organic fertilizers, but the marketplace also offers inorganic (chemical) fertilizers, mostly derived through fossil-fuel consumption. In general, organic fertilizers release the nutrients more slowly and promote long-term plant growth, whereas chemical ones provide a blast of nutrients that are used up quickly. You might liken it to a sugar- and fat-laden fast-food meal versus a balanced, whole-food-oriented, home-cooked one. Also, many chemical fertilizers are formulated for specific needs and do not offer a broad range of nutrients, whereas organic ones may contain a balance of primary, secondary, and micronutrients.

Compost is one of the best organic sources of nutrients, and it is the principal way to add organic matter to your soil. You can't boost organic matter of your soil by applying fertilizer. The added organic matter provided by compost *can* increase the CEC of the soil, but you won't know that definitively—or whether the compost also has increased your soil's nutrient levels—until you follow up with another soil test.

Like other organic soil amendments, compost releases nutrients slowly, as soil organisms break it down and its elements are adsorbed onto soil particles for use. Other organic materials, such as composted manure, grass clippings, chopped-up cover crops, or meals (a coarsely ground material, similar to cornmeal) made from seeds or animal by-products, will also have slow to moderate rates of availability. These various products can be used in combination with compost to address specific soil deficiencies discovered in your soil test. Bone meal, for instance, is high in phosphorus, whereas kelp meal or wood ashes boost potassium levels. Your soil test indicates the coverage rate at which you should apply these materials to adequately increase nutrient levels.

If you use fertilizer, the form of it is important, especially for winter gardeners. *Granular* fertilizer, whether organic or chemical, won't work in cold soils, because it needs microorganisms to break it down into elements the plants can use, and soil microbe activity plummets with decreasing soil temperature. There are other ways, such as liming the soil and using liquid fertilizer, to combat that situation.

In the late summer, *liming the soil* a week or two before planting fall and winter vegetables brings the CEC action back up to get winter crops off to a good start. When you add lime to the soil, you are fertilizing, because you're adding calcium and possibly magnesium (if your soil test recommends that you use dolomite lime). The calcium is said to sweeten the soil because it makes it less acidic. However, if your soil has a fairly neutral pH, you won't need to sweeten the soil. In that case, gaining trace amounts of calcium and magnesium through compost or selected organic fertilizers may be all that is necessary, and the addition of lime is not needed. I do not lime my garden every year; with a healthy level of organic matter in the soil and a regular infusion of compost, liming might be necessary only once every three or four years.

Although I might not add lime, if I want to fertilize my fall and winter plantings, I turn to *worm castings* or *liquid fertilizer* applied at transplanting time or possibly once shortly after planting. Worm castings, coming as they do from the warm, active worm bin, have a high level of microbial activity, so nutrients break down at a faster rate even in cooler soil. Liquid fertilizer, whether sprayed onto the foliage or watered into the soil around the plants, provides an immediate level of soluble nutrients.

How Much and When to Fertilize?

It's natural to apply fertilizer when getting the beds ready for plants in the spring, but what do you do after that? For years, it was a mystery to me how much fertilizer my plants were using, how often to fertilize them, and when enough was enough. When I began to grow vegetables year-round, however, I realized it was a question in need of an answer.

What I found was that some plants need more fertilizer than others. *Rodale's Encyclopedia of Organic Gardening,* the bible for backyard growers, explains that "some crops are heavy feeders, taking up large amounts of nutrients as they grow, while others are light feeders." So knowing the appetite of your favorite vegetables will help you plan a fertilization schedule. Studying university extension publications, information from fertilizer companies, and seed catalogs can give more detailed recommendations, but here are some general rules.

Most of the leafy greens are light feeders, not surprisingly. But many of our favorite root crops, such as carrots, onions, and beets, are too. Heavy feeders include the big vining vegetables of summer—potatoes, tomatoes, and squash—but also the brassicas that produce dense flower heads: broccoli and cauliflower. Spinach, although it's a leafy green, is a heavy feeder. Legumes (beans and peas) are light feeders but also have the ability to grab their own nitrogen out of the atmosphere and store it in their roots. What they don't need gets released back into the soil if you chop up and dig those roots into the soil, so these plants actually add fertilizer to your soil rather than just depleting it.

Also, different vegetables may use more of one type of nutrient than another. That is easy to understand when you think about nitrogen, because it is a prime factor in leafy green growth. If you want a plant to fill out with leaves, make sure it has enough nitrogen. However, if the plant is at its fruiting stage or you want it to go to seed, you don't want to promote leaf growth, so back off on the nitrogen. Lettuce likes nitrogen, a fruit crop such as tomatoes will benefit from phosphorus, and potassium is more in demand by such root crops as beets.

Considering all those factors, fertilizing vegetables for fall and winter can become a bit clearer. First, think about the feeding level of your plant. If your soil test showed medium to high levels of primary nutrients, don't worry about much fertilizer when growing lettuce, Swiss chard, Asian greens, or kales. Ditto with overwintering carrots, beets, and parsnips. Pay more attention to providing extra nutrition for fall or overwintering broccoli, Brussels sprouts, and cabbage.

When winter arrives, I stop applying fertilizer. Between November and February, plant growth slows as the plants harden themselves to survive the coldest months. Part of the process involves ceasing vegetative growth. If I were to feed them, the flush of available nitrogen might cause them to put on tender new growth in a brief spurt of sunny, warm weather, but that new growth would be the most susceptible to cold damage because the plant would not have had time to harden those tissues. It's better that I let the plants focus on toughening up to protect themselves from dropping temperatures and desiccating winds. So I wait, let them slumber in the coldest months, and begin fertilizing after growth starts again in late February or early March.

ROTATE CROPS FOR FERTILITY

Another way to ensure that your plants have adequate nutrients is through crop rotation. By alternating plantings of heavy feeders with light feeders, you don't tax the soil nutrient levels as greatly. By rotating plants with different nutrient needs into the same soil, you draw down the overall nutrient levels more slowly without having major deficiencies in any one. The overall effect is twofold: you can get by with using less fertilizer and adding it less frequently, and your soil health will be continually stable.

A common way of planting in rotation is to consider what part of the plant you eat, then rotating according to that. The rotation rhyme goes like this: "leaf, root, flower, fruit."

By rotating your crops—that is, planting leafy vegetables one season, followed by root vegetables, then flowering, then fruiting ones—you make your soil healthier and give your plants the nutrients they need. A big additional benefit is reduction of insect and disease problems, too, which comes when you consider rotation by plant family.

It's a Family Affair

You might not guess from the edible parts, but tomatoes and potatoes are in the same botanical family, Solanaceae, also known as the nightshade family. Peppers and eggplant are other commonly grown nightshades. Rotating those plants into the same garden spot in successive years would be unwise because, as *Rodale's* also tells us, "susceptibility to pests and diseases runs in plant families."

It might be a good practice to never replant the same family in the same place, but because most urban garden spaces are small, it's not a realistic idea. Common advice is to leave at least two years between using that same plot of land for plants of the same family. Three to seven years is preferred.

It also turns out that tomatoes are heavy feeders, so they suck up more soil nutrients than other crops. That affects what gets planted next in their spot. A light feeder such as a salad green might be a good choice. When the tomatoes come out at the end of summer, a winter crop of hardy greens could take their place.

Using the "leaf, root, flower, fruit" progression can balance out the nutrient needs and what is most likely available in the soil. Tomatoes fall into the fruit category and greens, of course, in the leaf category. So by planting greens in last year's tomato spot, you're practicing crop rotation.

After the winter greens are done, it's time for a root crop: perhaps beets or carrots, but not potatoes. A spring beet crop could be harvested by midsummer, at which time you might decide to let this plot of land rejuvenate. Plant a flowering cover crop to complete the rotation.

Some Susceptible Plant Families

Along with the nightshade family (Solanaceae: tomato, potato, eggplant, pepper, and tomatillo), other popular vegetable families that are especially in need of rotation include the mustards (Brassicaceae: broccoli, Brussels sprouts, cabbage, kale, and Asian greens), squashes (Cucurbitaceae: summer and winter squash, cucumbers, and pumpkins), and onions (Alliaceae: garlic, shallots, and leeks). These each can harbor their own particular soil-borne pests and diseases that may get worse year after year if the plants are grown in the same place for more than one season.

For instance, the larger brassicas attract garden pests, such as cabbage maggots, that can build up to unhealthy populations in the soil. The larvae stay in the soil or nearby plant material if they have a regular, preferred food source. A disease such as club root, a mold that affects the roots of brassicas, also remains in the soil once established. The cucurbits are susceptible to powdery mildew, which also may overwinter in the soil. Onions, which are susceptible to a number of soil-dwelling fungi, should be rotated for the same reasons. If other crops not bothered by the disease are planted in that soil for a couple of years, the particular problem should not build up.

Legumes to the Rescue

You can further boost soil health by becoming friends with the Leguminosae family. Legumes—beans and peas—have fewer problems than many vegetables, and planting them can actually improve the soil. Many legumes will "fix" nitrogen in the soil by pulling it from the air and storing it in their roots.

Instead of depleting nitrogen from the soil, like many leaf and fruit crops, legumes will at the very least leave the nitrogen level as is and possibly improve it. Growing legumes as cover crops, then digging the roots and chopped plants into the soil, releases that extra nitrogen, where it is available for the next crop.

In the rotation mantra of "leaf, root, flower, fruit," replace "flower" with "legume" to ensure an extra soil boost between other plantings.

If all that sounds daunting, as though pests and diseases lurk beneath the leaves of every plant sheltering its tiny plot of the soil, take heart. These practices are guidelines, and nature is somewhat forgiving. Simply applying some of these concepts, though, can increase the chances of healthy soil and bountiful gardens.

PROTECT AND SERVE SOIL WITH COVER CROPS

By now it should be clear that I believe a gardener's job is to feed the earth before asking that soil to feed him or her. To develop new garden beds and build the soil, you can sow a cover crop of legumes, small grains, or even annual flowers and let the soil rest beneath their green covering and light feeding habit. The next season, the cover crop can be chopped down and dug in before vegetable gardening begins.

Along with building the soil, a cover crop protects it against winter rains, smothers weed seeds, feeds soil organisms, and generates fertilizer that is useful in spring.

Cover crops are primarily legumes (such as fava beans, Austrian field peas, crimson clover, and vetch) or cereal grains (such as rye). Often they're mixed for sowing. They're widely available at nurseries and by mail order but probably least costly if purchased in bulk at feed stores in rural areas. Thrifty gardeners can use edible greens such as arugula or fast-growing flowers such as calendula, from which they can gather free seed. Your choice could be dictated by taste or practicality.

Crimson clover has beautiful flowers that bumblebees love, and it is easy to chop down and dig in. Hairy vetch offers *extrafloral nectaries,* nectar openings on its stems that feed beneficial insects

White nitrogen nodules are visible on the roots of this legume.

well before most flowers are open in the spring. To support the vetch's vining habit, grow it with tall, sturdy rye.

Consider the garden's next crop when planting the cover. If the bed will have peas or beans in it, plant a flowering cover rather than legumes. If the bed will have a heavy-feeding crop on it next, the nitrogen-fixing legumes may be just the ticket.

Timing might limit your choice, too. Some cover crops, such as crimson clover, are most productive if sown by the end of September, but you still might have your summer crops in the ground. Therefore, seeds such as fava beans, Austrian field peas, rye, and vetch, which can germinate in very cool weather, might be the best choice.

How It Helps

The primary benefits from cover crops happen belowground: the soil gains nitrogen, a better structure, and greater biological activity. "If you grow legumes, they will 'fix' nitrogen in the soil, and you can reduce the amount of fertilizer in the spring," explains Craig Cogger, soil scientist for Washington State University's Research and Extension Center in Puyallup. "You may be able

FALL COVER CROPS

Listed are fall cover crops commonly grown in the maritime Northwest. Expect less germination or ground coverage if sowing after planting dates.

CROP	TYPE	PLANTING DATES	SEED AVAILABILITY	WINTERKILL
Austrian field peas	Legume	early Sept.–late Oct.	Maybe	Occasional
Annual ryegrass	Grain	late Aug.–mid-Sept.	Common	Seldom
Cereal rye	Grain	late Aug.–late Oct.	Common	None
Crimson clover	Legume	late Aug.–mid-Sept.*	Common	Seldom
Fava (faba) bean	Legume	late Sept.–late Oct.	Common	Seldom
Vetch (common, hairy)	Legume	late Aug.–late Sept.*	Common	Seldom
Winter wheat	Grain	late Sept.–late Oct.	Maybe	Seldom

* These crops can be planted until mid-October in Oregon's Willamette Valley.
Source: WSU Extension, Seattle Tilth, regional garden centers

Fava beans and vetch cover crops

to reduce by one-third to one-half the amount of nitrogen you need to add."

Legumes attract soil-dwelling bacteria that attach to the plant's roots and pull atmospheric nitrogen out of the air and soil, storing it on the roots as white nodules. The plant feeds that bacteria with energy and nutrients, and the bacteria reward it with usable nitrogen. As the plant matures, it uses up some of the nitrogen, but when it is cut down and chopped up to decompose in the garden bed, the unused nitrogen remains in the soil to feed the leafy growth of other plants.

What to Do

All those benefits, yet cover crops require very little care. If sown early enough (see the Fall Cover Crops sidebar), cover crops will gain a few inches of growth before winter. If sown too early, the crop can get too large, which exposes it to winterkill, because it has too much tender new growth or is storing too much moisture in its cells. The best-

Straw mulch covers a bed cleared too late to plant cover crops, while cloche hoops wait for use.

timed cover crops fully cover the soil but are not tall or rangy; in early spring, they take off in a blaze of growth, and crops such as clover, fava, and vetch begin to flower. About that time, chop them down, triggering the third benefit to your soil: the addition of your vegetative fertilizer, known as green manure. Don't wait until the crop gets much older and past the flower stage, though, as the quality of this living fertilizer drops off, and the plants get woodier and more difficult to dig into the soil or, worse, go to seed and cause a weed problem.

At the cutting stage is where the work comes in. You didn't have to haul in yards of compost to improve your soil last fall—you just sprinkled a little seed. But in spring, it's time to put in the work.

Early spring is the best time to dig the cover crop into the soil, because that dose of green biomass is at its peak before the plants mature. If you have too much biomass, skim off half of it for your compost pile and dig in the rest. The chopped materials will start a riot of biological activity in your soil, and after a few weeks of decomposition, your energized soil will be ready for vegetable seeds and starts.

A MULCH FOR ALL SEASONS

One final way to build your soil and keep it energized for year-round growing: incorporate mulch into your repertoire. Mulch is a topdressing of organic material laid on top of the garden soil,

Twigs, leaves, weeds, and prunings can be sandwiched between wire grids to create a compost fence.

either when the soil is dormant or around existing plants. Either way, it helps build the soil, keep down weeds, and protect the garden from the weather.

We've already established how valuable it is to shield your garden soil from the maritime Northwest rains that will compact it and leach fertilizers and nutrients. If you are growing year-round, your plants can serve as that shield against the rain, but if your winter beds have a lot of open space around the crops (a good cultural method to not overtax the soil), you might want to mulch around them. In this situation, the mulch will also serve as a warming blanket around your winter crops, minimizing the effects of harsh winds and protecting against cold snaps and frost.

Many materials are used as mulch, but my favorites are straw, dried leaves, burlap bags, arborist chips, and compost.

Straw is used to keep down weeds and protect the soil from the elements. It's important to not get hay by mistake. Both are dry, baled products from a farmer's fields of small grains, but straw is just the shaft of the plant, whereas hay still has the seed heads attached. A layer of hay on your garden soil will quickly turn into a robust bed of alfalfa or whatever crop was used to make the hay. Straw has no seed heads. The relatively large, stiff shafts of straw cover the soil comprehensively and break down slowly. I break apart a bale and stick hand-fuls of straw 1–2 inches thick around my winter brassicas or between beds of row crops such as lettuces, carrots, or beets. Mature root crops can be mulched with straw right up to their crowns, although they should be monitored periodically to make sure there isn't too much moisture accumulating around the crown and causing rot to begin.

Dried leaves can be collected in the fall and stored in large bags or compost bins until needed. Don't have big trees on your land? Visit neighbors or volunteer to clean the leaves off the sidewalks of neighborhood schools. Leaves have many uses. I mix the brown leaves with green garden clippings into my compost, and I also lay a generous layer of leaves inside my worm bin as bedding and winter insulation. In the garden, leaves can be laid in a 2- to 4-inch-thick layer on top of beds and around plants in the same way as straw. To get smaller material that will stay in place better, leaves can be piled and run over with a lawn mower or put in a bucket and chopped up with a string weeder. Leaves can also be made into a nutritious compost, known as leaf mold. Simply pile leaves into a covered compost bin and let them sit for at least two years. The result will be a crumbly mulch.

I often use leaves to mulch my garlic from planting time in late October until early February, when I begin to see the garlic putting on height. At that time, I pull the leaves away and keep them at least a couple of inches from each plant, as I want the plants and the soil to dry out a bit to prevent white rot on the roots.

Burlap bags, currently a by-product of the booming artisan coffee movement, have grown to have multiple uses in Northwest gardens. Seek burlap bags out at local roasting plants or coffee shops run by the roasting company. You can lay them directly on your bare garden bed to reduce compaction from the rains and keep weeds at bay in winter. I've often seen them laid down as a path material in community gardens, and I use them to cover my compost pile, a technique that holds in heat and moisture as the compost cooks. The bags won't add any nutrients to your soil, but the natural materials recycle easily. Their fibers eventually break down, and when they get too stringy or fragmented, it's best to toss them onto the compost pile or into the garbage. Municipal composters sometimes ask residents not to put the bags into their yard-waste bins because the tough fibers can get caught in their industrial machinery.

Arborist chips, clippings from tree pruning run through a chipper, are my favorite free mulch. It takes a bit of legwork to find an arborist whose truck has just been filled and needs to be dumped, but if you have room for a big pile in your driveway, you will feel fortunate to make that connection. Tree companies have to pay to dispose of their clippings, so you save them money if you take it off their hands. However, most of the arborists I've contacted want to dump only a full load, so it's tricky to catch them at the right time. Also, make sure they haven't been chipping any diseased trees, something you wouldn't want to introduce to your yard. Recently, more homeowners have caught on to this good deal, and some tree companies in my area have begun charging a dumping fee. I prefer to trade a good load of chips for the traditional compensation of a six-pack of beer or soda, but it's a valuable commodity to me, so I might be persuaded to pay. I use a 4- to 6-inch-thick layer for path material and a thinner layer of 1–2 inches around perennials, trees, and shrubs, including around my perennial vegetables, herbs, and berries. Arborist chips will decompose over one to two years and need to be replenished.

Compost, whether from your own home bin or a commercial source, is a nutrient-rich

Make Your Own Compost

When you pull the old, spent plants from your vegetable garden, where do they go? Many people pack them into a yard-waste container and set it out at the curb for municipal pickup. That's OK for some things, such as large woody materials and diseased plants, but if you dispose of all your yard clippings, you're missing out on a satisfying homegrown recycling project: making your own compost.

Keep your spent garden plants at home, and you reduce the trucking needed to haul it off and, to some degree, the amount of compost you'll have to purchase, which has to be hauled in to your neighborhood supplier. You also can reduce your cash outlay from that purchase, because, once you've set up a bin, home composting costs nothing, except your labor.

Composting can be as simple as piling your yard waste into a heap in a back corner of the yard. Decomposition happens faster if you put it in a bin of some sort and turn it regularly. It also looks tidier in a bin, which can be made of welded wire formed into a cage, a wood frame with wire walls, or a fully enclosed wood bin with slats that have gaps wide enough to allow air movement. Some people use concrete blocks for bins; others purchase commercially made enclosures, often made with recycled plastic.

The most successful compost bin decomposes your material fast enough so that you can keep feeding it and use finished compost regularly. That requires "hot" composting, which involves techniques that encourage a heavy colonization of microorganisms in the pile, thus heating it up and decomposing it faster.

A hot compost system has a one-to-one ratio of materials rich in nitrogen (N) and carbon (C) in a pile large enough to trap heat, typically 3 feet by 3 feet by 3 feet. Combine equal parts N (fresh green material) and C (dry brown material), chop it into small chunks, water regularly, and flip the mixture between two bins periodically. The material will break down and become a stable, usable soil amendment in less than a season. If you're really energetic with it, you could have compost in three to four weeks.

A "cold" compost system takes less attention but makes compost much more slowly. Simply toss all yard waste into the bin as it's generated, and water it occasionally. It may take a year to make compost that way, but it is still keeping a precious resource at home and helping to close the loop on your gardening practices.

Save bags of autumn leaves and prunings from trees and shrubs, and get bags of untreated sawdust from a local carpenter. Have the neighbor kid dump freshly mown grass on your pile, and grab big bags of spent coffee grounds from the local espresso stand to add a jolt of nitrogen and get the pile heating up. Always chop new material into the bin as soon as you pull it from the garden, and toss a layer of leaves on top of it. Don't include kitchen scraps with meat, fish, or dairy in your compost bin, as it can result in a nasty smell and attract rodents to the pile.

This wine barrel makes an eye-catching worm bin.

the loop on your gardening practices and reduce your purchases (see the Make Your Own Compost sidebar).

Tending your soil from season to season—checking off those tasks such as soil testing, fertilizing, crop rotation, cover-cropping, and mulching—is a process that pays healthy dividends into your food garden account. By building the soil and keeping it fertile, you make it possible to get more productivity out of your garden beds and put food on your table throughout the year.

product of yard clippings and other organic materials. Applied as a topdressing, compost has nutrients that eventually will be drawn down into the bed by soil-dwelling organisms or water. If you have healthy soil and practice crop rotation, compost could provide most, if not all, of your fertilizer needs. Compost also can improve the tilth of the soil, giving it better structure and water-holding ability. Used as a topdressing, however, it can initially crust over and create a hydrophobic condition in which water just runs off. If that happens, simply cultivate the soil lightly once and it likely will be fine thereafter. Using your garden clippings for home compost can be a rewarding way to close

COOL-SEASON KEYS TO SOIL BUILDING

- Test your soil every few years to monitor its fertility.
- Understand that plants need more than just N-P-K.
- Aim at care and feeding of the entire "soil food web."
- Reduce fertilizer needs by crop rotation and cover cropping.
- Reduce pests and diseases in soil by rotation of plant families.
- Mulch to protect the soil, warm it, and suppress weeds.
- Close the loop by making your own compost.

5

Planting
Seeds and Starts

Down in my basement sits the secret to a great edible garden. It's not a fancy tool or magic growth elixir. It's a few boxes of seeds, with rectangular, palm-sized store-bought packets and jars of home-saved seeds all lined up by plant family and kept cool, dry, and in the dark until use.

I feel about my seed collection the way my friend and cowboy poet D. W. Groethe must have felt when he waxed poetic about seeing his ranch-hand girlfriend in a new outfit of heavy cotton work clothes: "Inside that brown duck / is most of my luck!" Those little boxes hold gardens full of my luck, in the form of many future meals. I just have to nudge them into life by mixing them with a bit of soil and water and getting them out into the light.

Well, perhaps the enterprise is a bit more complex than that, but not much. Growing plants from seeds is one of the most basic acts of civilization, one enacted quite handily for many centuries before the study of botany unpacked the mystery of life sprouting from seeds and the practice of agriscience gave us a plethora of new tools to help the process along.

Spring starts early for me, even though it's still verifiably winter just outside the window when I venture down into the basement, pull out the seed boxes, and plant the first seeds into flats indoors.

STARTING SEEDS INDOORS

Starting seeds in flats—trays with small "cells" that you fill with a special seedling soil blend—is a satisfying late-winter activity, and it can greatly boost your spring garden bounty. It's wonderful to have a little forest of riotous leaves from a particularly robust batch of seeds that you perhaps planted a little too thickly in your zeal. No problem, as you can easily quell the riot in cell block number nine: just take a tiny pair of scissors and snip off all but one or two seedlings at the soil level so the plants don't get stunted because of overcrowding.

Besides the seed trays and seedling soil blend, you'll need a heat source to warm the soil in your little pots and supplemental lighting to get the seedlings off to a strong start once they've emerged from the soil. The entire seed-starting arrangement described below—because it is nearly self-sufficient with light and heat—can be placed in an out-of-the-way location, such as a heated basement or utility room.

Seed packets often give guidelines for starting indoors versus planting directly in the garden bed, usually tying their recommendations to "X number of weeks before the last frost date." Once I've done that calculation (see Frosty the Forecaster in chapter 2), I pull out my seed-starting supplies.

When starting seeds indoors, consider the amount of available space. It may be easy to find a space for a seed flat, but you could get dozens of plants from one sowing. If these will need to be potted up into larger pots and kept indoors, also think about the amount of space those would take up. I always seem to plan for fewer plants than I want to tend and then end up with more than what I'd expected. A heated greenhouse could take the place of these other extras (see chapter 8).

Propagation Boxes

For indoor seed starting in winter, most gardeners in maritime climates need supplemental heat and light. (Midsummer sprouting of fall and overwintering vegetables can be done outdoors and has a different set of challenges, as covered in chapter 6.) In winter, warming the soil or seed-starting mix will boost germination for some crops. Once the seedlings are up and reaching for the sky, they'll need more help, because weak winter sun and many cloudy days do not provide enough solar radiation to get them off to a good, strong start. Also, the shorter days of winter do not provide enough hours of light to grow seedlings at the optimum rate.

Therefore, a propagation setup is advisable; it consists of an electric heating mat, seed trays, and grow lights (see Seed-Starting Shelves in the Appendix). If you are not interested in putting together your own seed-starting apparatus and have a bit of disposable income, you could purchase a commercial propagation station. Designs run from simple to clever and can easily cost well over one hundred dollars. But for that, you get a complete system that you just have to assemble. Some models have handy extras, such as shelves designed to perfectly fit multiple flats, stands on rollers, and even larger ones with plastic zip-off covers that could be used in a protected outdoor location.

Heat Mats

A heat mat is an electric coil inside a waterproof pad that is plugged into a wall outlet and placed

---

------------------ *Why Start with Seeds?* ------------------

Starting from seed provides benefits ranging from a wider choice of varieties to sturdier plants.

- **Get growing earlier:** you won't find seedlings of some crops in the nurseries until near the time they can be planted out in your area.
- **More choice of varieties:** hundreds of seed catalog listings far surpass the few common varieties grown commercially as starts—and you can delight friends with your finds!
- **Some just don't work as starts:** root crops, especially, do not transplant well, so must be started from seed in the garden.
- **More control over conditions:** you can be assured your seeds are grown organically, with materials such as a seed-starting mix that meets your requirements.
- **More sustainable practices:** recycling old pots and buying seed packets rather than plants reduces your "consumer-use profile," a combination of carbon footprint, packaging, and waste.

under a seed tray to radiate heat up into the soil of a seed flat. It's safe to water seedlings in trays sitting on a heat mat, but be careful not to let this electrical product get in too much contact with water.

The heat mat is designed to heat the soil in seed flats 15°F–20°F above room temperature. It helps to attach a thermostat, usually purchased separately, that can be set at the target temperature. The goal is to warm the soil enough to trigger germination and get the plants off to a vigorous start. Seeds need different temperatures at which to germinate (see the Indoor Germination Temperatures for Cool-Season Vegetables sidebar later in this chapter), and often it is not possible to get a consistent, effective temperature from soil in a seed flat on the floor or pots on a windowsill. The exception might be a house with radiant floor heating, especially if the floor is finished concrete or tile.

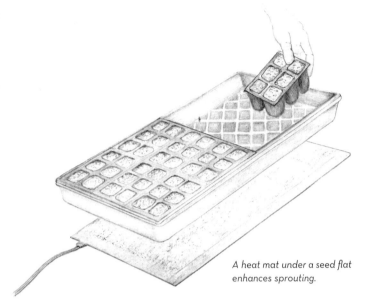

A heat mat under a seed flat enhances sprouting.

The old-fashioned way to sprout seeds is by putting the seed flat on a radiator, a radiantly heated floor, or even on top of the refrigerator, which in most cases is a consistently warm place where warm air from the motor often circulates, but the heat mat might be a more adaptable solution.

Seed Flats

The seed flat used on top of the mat often has a series of small cells that each contain one seedling. It also could be a collection of 2- or 4-inch pots with more than one seedling growing in each pot, or even an entire open flat just filled with soil, into which the seed is broadcast. The seed flat is perforated for drainage, but under it is a solid plastic tray to catch the water.

Recycled materials such as empty egg cartons also work to grow seedlings in. Although the gridded flats are quick and easy, there is satisfaction

Brassica and lettuce seedlings

from making your own seed-starting pots from newspaper or using renewable or biodegradable materials, also sold commercially.

You could also build sturdy wooden seed flats, fill them with soil, and randomly broadcast the seeds onto the soil, covering them lightly. This last method requires more delicate work when repotting, but it appeals to the more environmentally conscious gardener who wants to buy and store fewer commercial materials or reduce the amount of new plastic purchased.

Grow Lights

Once a seed has breached the soil, it also needs light for healthy growth. Unfortunately, midwinter in the maritime Northwest is not a very luminous experience. The days are short, the sun is often hidden by clouds, and on stormy days it can seem downright dim outside. So the level of light that seeps into our houses is likely not enough to keep up our spirits, much less our seedlings. For most of us, an additional light source is needed.

A fluorescent light is hung over the plants and kept a couple of inches above the seedlings as they grow. Lighting should be left on for fourteen to

sixteen hours per day, longer than even the strongest natural light source on our northern climate's late-winter days. Fluorescent is used rather than other lights because it emits very little heat, so it can be placed close to the plants, providing greater light intensity.

Gardeners debate whether specialized grow lights are necessary for seedlings, but it's well accepted that light intensity from fluorescents is much better than winter sunlight. Recently, smaller, lighter, and more energy-efficient bulbs have been developed that provide more intense light than standard 4-foot "shop bulbs." The trade-off is that they are also quite a bit more expensive.

The light is hung from a light-duty chain with small links so it can be raised regularly as the seedlings grow. A cord and pulleys or eye hooks with weights on the other end of the cord also work to hold the light at the right height.

Covers

Many seed-starting systems sold in nurseries today come with the undertray that holds water, the multicelled tray for soil and seeds, and a clear, domed top to act as a minigreenhouse (which also can be bought individually). The top holds in moisture, thereby increasing humidity and requiring less water. If you use a well-moistened starter mix when filling the tray and then cover it, it may be several days before you need to water again. Or cover the wetted seed tray with the stretchy plastic film that's used to store leftover food in the refrigerator. That provides a tight seal against evaporation, but it must be removed promptly when the seedlings appear. Pay close attention to soil moisture and humidity in the flat; lack of water is the surest ways to thwart germination or stunt or kill your new seedlings.

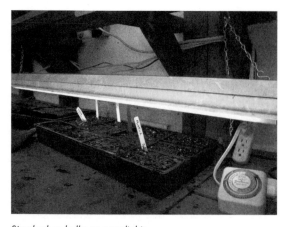

Simple shop bulbs as grow lights

Seed Starting Mixes

I either purchase a seed-starting soil mix or make my own. The commercial mixes have very little actual soil in them—they're a blend of peat, vermiculite, perlite, and other very lightweight materials that hold water, increase air space in the mix, and are easy for a seedling's roots to push through. When I shop for a commercial mix, I look for ones that do not contain peat or those additives, though.

Peat, sometimes called peat moss, is harvested from bogs. Although it is a renewable resource because it builds back up over time, that rebuilding is such a slow process that there is a concern about overuse. Other environmental concerns involve loss of wetland habitat when peat is harvested, and the value of peat bogs for storage of carbon dioxide, which would otherwise be released into the atmosphere and contribute to global warming.

Vermiculite and perlite provoke different concerns. Vermiculite is a mined mineral that has been found to be contaminated with asbestos also present in the mine. Because asbestos is carcinogenic if breathed into the lungs and seed-starting mixes are very dry and dusty, I do not want to take the chance that airborne asbestos fibers will come out of that mix.

Perlite, a type of volcanic rock that expands to many times its original size when dried by heating to high temperatures, does not pose the asbestos problems, but the mining process creates a fine airborne dust that can irritate the eyes and lungs. Perhaps perlite, or the round white polystyrene beads that are sometimes substituted for it, are necessary seed-starting additives for commercial growers, but I believe my home gardening efforts can do without them.

When I make my own seed-starting mix, it's half sterile compost and half coconut coir,

with perhaps a bit of sand. Coir, which is a more renewable material than peat and serves the same purpose, is made from ground-up coconut husks. In my experience, coir and peat have similar properties as a lightweight, water-holding soil extender and aerator.

I don't pull compost for the seed-starting mix from my own backyard bins—too much microbial activity and material breakdown is going on, which would compete for nutrients with my new seedlings. Also, there might be soil pathogens in homemade compost, such as harmful fungi or bacteria, and those could bloom if brought into a warm seed-starting environment. Some gardeners sterilize their home compost in a warm oven, but I just purchase a small amount of sterile commercial compost for starting seeds.

Seedling Care

Once most of the seedlings are up and growing, you can remove the supplemental heat source from beneath the flat.

Watering indoor seedbeds is a daily chore, and it requires diligence. As most seeds sprout, water is the only external input they need, although a few need light or some other special condition. The seed internally contains all the food it needs in its starchy casing, so fertilizer is not needed to feed a sprouting seed. Just water, on a regular basis.

Most seeds sprout best when the soil is kept moist on the surface, not allowed to dry to a lighter color, or, by the same token, not doused so much that water stands on the surface of the pot. Just as the soil surface begins to dry out, it must be replenished by giving it another drink.

If the seed flat has bottom heat, the soil will dry faster than you expect. I check my seedlings at least twice a day, morning and late afternoon, although if I'm around on a warm day, a lunchtime visit sometimes finds them in need of water, too. It seems as if you can't give too much attention to a sprouting seed.

Another challenge is too much moisture. Condensation or standing water around the stem can result in *damping off* disease, which is caused by a fungus. A seedling's stem will shrivel up just above the soil line, and the plant will topple over. To prevent damping off, remove the domed lid and make sure there is good air movement across the plants to dry the stems. I often blow on my seedlings after watering, which has additional benefits. The plants will respond to an influx of carbon dioxide from my breath, and it gets my face down close to the flat so I can clearly see how moist the soil is and how the plants are doing. Also, a bit of wind helps strengthen the stems and mimics outdoor conditions. A small fan set up at soil level to send wind across the flat accomplishes nearly the same purpose.

Damping off also can be avoided by watering from beneath, once the seedlings have enough roots to reach the bottom of their pots, and by carefully watering the surface of the soil to minimize splashing or drenching the stems. Use a watering can with a long stem and small spout. For very small seedlings, I use a plastic bicycle water bottle that I can squeeze to deliver just the right amount of water to each cell.

Once the seeds have grown a while, and especially after they've been "potted up" into 3- or 4-inch pots where they'll stay until planting out (see the next section), you might try a capillary mat (also called a moisture mat) under the pots inside the solid tray that catches excess water. You can buy the spongy material in a roll and cut it to fit inside those trays, with one end of it left long to overlap the end of the tray. The exposed end goes into a reservoir of water, and as moisture evaporates or is taken up by the plants, more is wicked

---

Indoor Germination Temperatures for Cool-Season Vegetables

Many cool-season vegetables sprout at temperatures lower than what we find comfortable in our homes, but they germinate more robustly at standard household temperatures. Seedlings prefer a consistent temperature in their first weeks of life, a detail to which we must pay attention if we have seedlings growing indoors and we lower our house thermostat at night.

Need Cool Weather (minimum germination temperature 40°F–45°F; optimum 55°F–65°F): lettuce, peas, chard, endive, mustards, wild greens, spinach

Want More Warmth (minimum germination temperature 50°F–55°F; optimum 60°F–75°F): broccoli, Brussels sprouts, cabbage, cauliflower, collards, kale, kohlrabi, leeks, onions

Not included in this list are root crops such as beets and carrots, because, even though they can be planted in the early spring or midspring seasons, they are generally sown directly into the soil rather than started indoors and transplanted out. Peas and spinach also do better if directly sown in the garden but can be started indoors. These outdoor-sown plants also have minimum germination temperatures (see the Growing in Seven Seasons chart in chapter 6).

into the mat from the reservoir. Plants draw up water as they need it, and because that eliminates watering on the soil surface, you can reduce the chance of damping off or fungal diseases attacking your seedlings. But for it to work, the plants must have a robust root system that can get to the water.

REPOTTING AND TRANSPLANTING SEEDLINGS AND STARTS

Transplanting is the next activity to schedule, and it comes two to four weeks after the seeds emerge. Once the seedlings have two or three sets of true leaves, I move them carefully into 3- or 4-inch pots. Later, it's time to harden them off and move them outdoors.

Get 'Em into Larger Pots

To transplant seedlings into larger pots, I've developed a few tricks.

1. **Water the seedlings ahead of time:** Make sure the seedling's soil is not too dry or too wet. Too dry, and soil will fall away from the roots; too wet, and it will slump. Either condition is hard on tender roots. A damp soil plug should keep its shape pretty well and protect the seedling's root system.

2. **Get the larger pots ready first:** Clean the pots with a mild water-bleach solution (sixteen-to-one ratio) to make sure you won't bring any pathogens into the house or onto your new plants. Rinse thoroughly and dry. Similarly, clean the seed trays that will hold the pots.

3. **Mix a slightly denser soil medium:** I use half sterile compost and half commercial potting soil for the larger pots.

4. **Fill each pot with soil:** Add soil to two-thirds full and make a hole in the center about the size of one seed-flat cell.

Grasp seedling by the cotyledon leaf.

5. **Carefully dislodge the seedlings:** Slide a straight, thin tool (I use a plastic picnic knife) around the edge of a seed-flat cell.

6. **Grasp the seedling gently by its cotyledon leaves:** The cotyledon leaves are also called the seed leaves, which are the first leaves to emerge from the seed and are not necessarily the shape of the plant's true leaves. They are expendable and will wither and die, anyway, so it's much better to hold the plant by these than by a true leaf or, worse, the stem.

7. **Pull the seedling out:** Slide a small tool (I often use a plastic picnic spoon) into the bottom of the cell and scoop up the entire cell's worth of soil and plant. For root-bound seedlings, turn the packet of cells upside down and tap or squeeze the soil block from the cell, but for the health of your plants, don't let them stay in the cells so long that they become root-bound (a mass of roots that crowds the pot; if you see this condition, loosen the root mass slightly when repotting).

8. **Place the seedling in the pot:** Carefully lower the clump of soil and plant into the hole in the larger pot.

A repurposed wood box serves as a seed bed for peas.

9. **Settle the seedling in the pot:** Steadying the plant with one hand, slip soil in around its base until the plant is snug in place. Do not let soil rise above the original root level. (One exception is tomatoes: through "adventitious rooting," they will develop new roots at the leaf nodes if their stems are buried in soil as they're repotted or planted into the ground; it's beneficial, as the plant will develop a much stronger root system.)
10. **Water lightly and slowly:** Watch the plant settle into its new home. If air pockets appear, slip in a little more soil.
11. **Label the new pot:** It's surprisingly easy to get mixed up when you're potting up more than one variety of a particular vegetable, so label them as you do each one.

Get 'Em Out the Door

Seed propagation is naturally only the first step in the process. Your healthy vegetable starts need to be transplanted into the garden in the proper method at the right time. Timing is crop-dependent, and a general guideline for each vegetable can be found in the listings in chapter 9.

Often, early-spring crops start life in a seedbed for two to three weeks. After that, I pot them up into 4-inch pots and let them develop their roots for another two to three weeks before beginning the process of getting them into the ground. Although you may be ready to get all these plants out of your house after five to six weeks, it's important to introduce them slowly to the outdoors. You can't just march outside one sunny day, pot in hand, and plop the indoor-grown seedling into the ground. It needs to be acclimated to the weather conditions it will find in the garden. The crucial step before transplanting is called "hardening" (or sometimes "hardening off").

Indoor plants have been pampered by a consistent temperature and air movement, but when they get outside, they will be bombarded by gusting winds and temperature fluctuations when the sun comes out or goes behind clouds. Also, they will need to survive in much colder nighttime temperatures. Therefore, gardeners harden the young plants by exposing them to small bouts of outdoor weather, then slowly increasing that exposure over a week or so. Working up from two or three hours to a full day reduces transplant shock.

You can also continue the hardening process by leaving the plants out overnight in a cloche or cold frame in their pots. They can, with regular watering, live a number of days in this situation if necessary, and the extra protection of being under cover could protect them from unusually cold nights as opposed to planting them in uncovered ground. But I've never found that it helps the growth to extend their time in pots once they are ready to go into the ground. Once you have taken the seedlings through the hardening process, it's better to leave the plants outside under cover rather than to continue to bring them in overnight.

Get 'Em Growing in the Beds

When moving the plants from pot to bed, be mindful again of the stress that places on the roots, and the rest of the plant, for that matter. Use the right-sized tool (my favorite is the hori-hori, a Japanese garden knife) to scoop them carefully from the pot, bringing as much soil with the plant in one unit as possible. Again, don't transplant when the pots are too dry or too wet.

It also helps to plan the transplant when the weather is cooperative. Don't choose a very warm day when the sun is blazing overhead or a blustery day when a gale or rainstorm is raging. A cloudy, cool day is best, and late in the day is also good, because the plant will have closed off its stomata, which it uses to respire (breathe). In this resting state and not taxed by the elements, it will suffer less transplant shock.

After transplanting into the beds, water lightly; if unusually cool weather is predicted, erect a temporary cover to protect the plant, remembering to remove it the next day so it doesn't cook in the sun.

A temporary covering is just one way to help get your plant growing well once it's transplanted into its final home. Whether early-spring planting helps get a jump on summer, or early-fall planting extends the growing season through autumn, you are putting those plants into a more stressful situation than they'd have in the reliable summer weather. Besides season-extending techniques, here are a few other ways to ensure successful transplanting:

- **Increase spacing when planting out.** For instance, if the standard spacing for a plant is 4 inches, give it 6; if the standard is 8 inches, give it 10–12.
- **Thin after planting out.** Use double spacing for root crops, and a bit wider spacing than normal for greens.
- **Weed religiously.**

These techniques ensure that your transplant—whether you grew it from seed or bought starts—will have less competition for soil nutrients at root level. This is an important consideration for growing during the cooler seasons, when soil microbe activity is lower and thus fewer nutrients are available.

Healthy plants grow from well-sprouted seeds and carefully tended starts. It's a process that gives the gardening year a glorious start. For the cool-season gardener, the steps are repeated periodically throughout the year to keep growing year-round. Whatever the season, careful attention—and perhaps your own bit of brown-duck luck—will turn the tiny vessels of edible DNA into delicious, nutritious garden produce.

COOL-SEASON KEYS TO PLANTING SEEDS AND STARTS

- Begin earlier by starting seeds indoors.
- Presprout seeds for quicker germination.
- Start seeds in a propagation box—just add heat and light.
- Repot and harden seedlings before planting outdoors.
- Protect transplanted seedlings and starts.

Part II

Becoming a
Cool-Season
Gardener

6

Expanding Your Seasonal Perception

When I first started growing food, I'd wait for spring, looking forward to the day when I could run down to the nursery, fill a couple of shallow cardboard boxes with plant starts, then cart them back to the garden and plant them. I expanded my repertoire by growing some things from seed—beets, carrots—that I didn't see in 4-inch pots but could find in the seed racks. Then I realized that not every plant likes the same conditions, so I would need to start planting things in series, first getting the vegetables that can handle the cooler weather and waiting for a few weeks to get the warm-season vegetables.

That's still a passable plan for a summer gardener in the maritime Northwest, but our climate allows us so much more opportunity. I dig through my seed packets on a weekly basis, fiddling with seedbeds and transplants during six or seven key periods throughout the year, and at any given time I am tending plants at many different growth stages. I constantly keep an eye on the calendar, with a goal to be able to pull some food from my garden year-round. Through repetition year after year, some of the practices have become second nature, but there are still times when I need a reminder of what to plant, when to plant it, and how to figure out the best cycle for my garden's life. As I recorded my practices and gathered additional information for this book, I was surprised to find how much there is to think about and keep track of. The cycle of seeding, transplanting, potting up, sowing in succession, interplanting, and all the peripheral tasks of the year-round gardener starts in late winter and shakes me out of the frigid doldrums. After that awakening, it's full speed ahead for nearly the whole year.

RETHINKING THE CALENDAR

Spring, summer, autumn, winter—anyone can look at the almanac and say yep, those are our seasons, for better or worse; always have been. But I am a modern American who is used to more of everything, and four just does not seem like enough. So I've devised a way to get more seasons out of a year. It's a complicated system based on lunar phases, calendars from ancient peoples, and the teachings of … well, no it isn't. I'll confess. Wanting to tend my garden continually throughout the year in our mild climate has made me chop up our seasons into a few "miniseasons" so I can more easily plan and plant. I still get the same seasons as everybody else, but it just seems like more. In this chapter I describe the traits of my seven growing seasons for the maritime Northwest and provide my list of what to plant when.

Lucky Seven

For a couple of years I taught skiing at a day area in the Cascades, and the school's dynamic leader, John Mohan, loves skiing so much that he called himself, and us, the "Lucky Dogs" for being able to be out there regularly enjoying such a fabulous sport. I didn't disagree, except for those times when the lure of the snow was outdone by the lure of the soil. At that point, taking the kids through the drills of making their skis into hot dog shapes (Go!) or pizza shapes (Stop!) was a distraction from making shapes of my own, like the green luge (a furrow for planting seeds, made with the blade of my hori-hori) or the hole-in-one (thumb-sized depression in a pot of soil for a seed or transplant). I heartily endorse John's concept of the Lucky Dog as someone doing something he or she loves, though now I just transfer it over to my gardening.

The way I approach growing food in our maritime Northwest climate, we have seven chances throughout the year to be Lucky Dogs. As a beginning gardener, you probably thought of "the season" as that perfect summer day when you can pluck ripe tomatoes off the vine while walking barefoot through the garden. Sure, that's one. But what about the misty morning when you pick a salad of a dozen ingredients for your Thanksgiving dinner table? Or when you snatch some peas off the vine while raking up the fall leaves, and the taste transports you back to the spring days of your youth? Or when you reach down through a foot of snow to cut a glossy, purple-veined head of savoy cabbage? Lucky, lucky, lucky you.

SEVEN SEASONS OF VEGGIES

How you get to harvest edibles year-round is by looking at the gardening calendar a little differently. Consider this breakdown, with dates listed for my Seattle garden, which would need to be adjusted a bit for your location, microclimate, and gardening practices.

Early Spring (Mid-February to Late March)

Early spring is a time to begin planting the first seeds of the season. "Plant peas by Presidents Day" used to be a common phrase in Cascadia, and some years it works great, whereas other years their sprouting and growth is much more reliable if you wait a couple of weeks, and later-planted ones will easily catch up with the earliest sowings. Success also depends upon your microclimate.

During early spring, the soil begins to stir with life. Raised beds are warmed by occasional sunny days, but the uncovered bed of garden soil will still drop below 40°F at night, which means most vegetable seeds will not sprout.

Chop up extra cover crops for your compost bin.

This is the time to begin "plasticulture" gardening by pulling out your crop covers to help you get started. With cover, the soil temperature will stabilize in the low 40s and outdoor planting can begin. Protection from temperature fluctuations, wind, and rain will greatly benefit tender young crops.

Midspring (Late March to End of May)

Midspring is a changeable period of glorious warm weekends and false starts, when we think summer has arrived, only to see it drowned or chilled back into remission. Often we get a burst of warmth in mid-May, only to be followed by "Junuary." But the good days provide the perfect time to tackle the weeds (they come out so easily when the ground is moist!) and chop in the cover crop, building the soil and readying it for production. Feed the perennial vegetables and fruits. Pull the mulch away from the crowns of the overwintered vegetables so the spring rains don't set those plants to rotting.

Veteran gardeners might resist getting their heat-loving summer crops into the ground just yet; there are so many other things to plant and more sowings to make of the earliest crops. This is the glory time for cool-season crops, when sprouting is easy. As nighttime soil temperatures reach 45°F in open ground and up to 50°F under season-extending covers, early crops spring forward like the clock at daylight saving time.

Use the occasional dreary days to sow and tend hot crops indoors and, toward the end of mid-spring, set the healthy transplants out after hardening, but keep them under cover. Also use season extension when you seed the tenderest hot crops into warmed, well-composted soil.

Late Spring (June to Mid-July)

That's right: you will be slaving over a hot barbecue grill on a late spring day known to all of America as Independence Day. Keep your fleece vest at hand. The calendar makers may put "first day of summer" in late June at solstice time, but it just doesn't happen that way for us in the maritime Northwest. Not reliably, anyway. Since I began training myself to think of spring ending on Bastille Day (off with its head!), I have been a much happier gardener.

My season-extending covers come off the cool-season crops as the soil stays in the low 50s at night, but I keep them on the warm-season vegetables through late spring, with adequate venting on warm days, of course. Many maritime Northwest areas begin to experience their first growing degree days (GDD) of the year during this season, which means enough warmth is accumulating for plants to put on consistent growth. (See Using a Better Calculation: Growing Degree Days in Chapter 2.)

Two layers of early spring protection: floating row cover topped by a small commercial plastic cloche

Helping Germination Along

My friend and excellent Seattle grower Amy Ockerlander swears by leaching carrot seeds for better germination. Although I've chitted potatoes, scarified beans and beets, and pre-sprouted (called greensprouting by the British) a lot of seeds, I hadn't tried this one.

"Carrot seeds are notoriously finicky about germinating," Amy tells me, "which is why I leach them before sowing. This process washes off the chemical substance that inhibits germi-nation, and they pop right out of the ground for me. It also makes it easier for me to sow the

Presprouting pea seeds will have them popping out of the soil in no time.

seeds, as they are swollen from soaking in water and I am able to sow them farther apart."

Leaching is similar to the other processes, which are all pretty easy. The science behind these germination-aiding techniques is a bit more complicated.

Plants have various ways of keeping their seeds from sprouting prematurely; it's likely that their seeds, produced at the end of a growing season, will not successfully produce new plants if the seeds immediately sprout and grow. Makes sense: the end of the growing season is generally followed by cold weather. If the seeds sprouted in the fall, the plants would just die with the onset of cold weather. So the seeds have built-in defenses, which gardeners can overcome with these special techniques to trigger germination.

Leaching: Soak the seeds overnight in a jar of water. The next day, drain the seeds into a fine mesh colander, rubbing the seeds vigorously while running water over them in the sieve. Cover them with a plastic bag, then repeat the rinsing and rubbing process a few hours later, and then a third time a few hours after that. Cover again with plas-tic and leave overnight, then plant the next day. Amy's technique hastens the natural process that would take place after you plant a seed. In a cou-ple of days, you'll mimic the effects of many days of rain or watering. Try it on long-sprouting seeds such as carrots, parsnips, turnips, and parsley. "Works like a charm!" she says.

Presprouting: Sandwich seeds between paper towels or coffee filters on a plate. Soak well with water. You can cover the plate with clear plastic cling wrap or slip it into a zip-close plastic bag if you are concerned about it drying out during the sprouting process. Check it regularly to keep it consistently moist. After a few days, the seeds will swell up and send out a small root. Then it's time to plant, being careful not to damage the delicate root when slipping the seed into the soil. Sometimes the roots will grab onto a paper towel, but they won't burrow through coffee filters. Some gardeners presprout many of their direct-sown seeds. Try it on lettuce, especially when sowing in midsummer, and on wrinkled seeds, like peas.

Chitting: This is simply the method of setting out potatoes and letting them sprout. Place the seed potatoes in an open container (an egg carton works great) in a warm location. Separating and spreading them out helps protect the tender shoots that will sprout from the eyes on the potato. Allow to grow until they're a couple of inches long, then carefully plant them. You might want to cut the potato into multiple pieces, leaving two or three shoots per piece.

Scarifying: Some seeds need to be roughed up a bit before they will sprout. A bit of scarring on their tough outer coatings will allow moisture in more quickly and trigger sprouting. This process mimics what happens in a bird's crop, in which food is passed through a sieve of gravel to help grind it up. You can do it by rubbing seeds over a piece of sandpaper or a metal file, just enough so you can see scratching on the surface. You can also just rub them in a handful of sand for a bit. Or it can be done with hot water, pouring boiling water over the seeds and letting them sit for a minute or so. Try it with spinach or beans.

A simple cold frame of plastic sheeting stretched over a wood frame

Summer (Mid-July to Mid-September)

It's cruel, isn't it, that Cascadia is graced with only two months of true summer? It's especially hard on those of us who grew up or moved here from places where the summer warmth hit early and stayed late, like a pack of old relatives on their first vacation in years. I remember t-shirt nights in North Dakota as a boy when we stayed outside playing in the heat long after darkness fell around 9:30 or 10:00 PM on the longest days of the year. Sadly, true native maritime Northwesterners might never have known such joys. By the time we finally get our truly warm spell, those daylight hours are already on the wane, making an al fresco dinner a bit dicey as the temperature drops with sundown.

But this is the prime growing period, the only time when our soggy climate truly dries out. The rains taper off to nothing, and widespread watering is needed throughout the garden as the zucchinis crawl toward the porch and cherry tomatoes plump up.

---------- *Snapshot: Ariadne Garden Journal* ----

The Ariadne Garden in Portland is a legacy of the late urban farmer Kim McDodge. Betty Barker, a Master Gardener who is one of a group that tends this garden, shares some journal entries from their 2010 plantings:

7/4	Start Lacinato kale in six-packs
7/26	Direct-seed Russo-Siberian kale, also chard and spinach in lots of compost
8/2	Transplant Lacinato kale
8/3	Start Winter Wonderland romaine lettuce in pots
8/6	Direct-seed Silverado chard
8/16	Thickly plant radicchio, to divide later
8/27	Plant black-seeded Simpson lettuce
8/30	Transplant Winter Wonderland romaine
9/3	Plant broccoli raab

Because this short summer is followed by a long, mild fall, plan a second sowing of some short-season crops for autumn harvest. Some hardier vegetables are able to weather the cooling nights just fine, but plan your plantings so that you can erect a cloche over the more tender fall crops as summer warmth fades, to extend their productive season.

This is also the time when we, alas, must set our sights on winter! If we want to eat well from our garden in the cool seasons to come, now is the time to rotate crops and sow long-season overwintering vegetables, taking the most care to keep them moist so that they get off to a proper start. Almost anything will sprout in soil that is consistently in the low 60s at the beginning of our maritime summer, but I keep an eye on the soil thermometer as evening temperatures begin to drop again.

Early Fall (Mid-September to Mid-October)

Wash the canning jars and buy new lids before the grocer runs out, because early fall is the prime harvest time, and you'll want to store up some summer abundance for the hungry months ahead. As fall temperatures set the trees to blushing, they also trigger warm-season crops to set their seed, which you can harvest and store as a thrifty, close-the-loop gardening practice (see the Save Your Own Seeds sidebar). Can, dry, freeze, cellar, make sauces and jams, and eat well at this most abundant time of the year.

The rains are also beginning again, and overwintering vegetables still to go in the ground must be shielded and warmed by season-extending devices. As summer and short-season fall crops come out, protect the beds that aren't getting another food crop with a sowing of quick-sprouting cover crops. These shield the soil from compaction by rain, provide winter habitat for critters in your ecosystem, and help build the soil for next year's planting.

Late Fall (Mid-October to Late November)

Year-round gardeners can truly fill a cornucopia with vegetable abundance from their own garden at Thanksgiving. It will be one of the great joys of your year-long effort. As you pull down the trellises and compost the wilted plants that fed you so well, you have one more harvest to take in. Reap the fruits from the second planting of vegetables that went in at the height of summer, and the fourth, fifth, or sixth successive crop of lettuces and other greens that grow so quickly in the cooler seasons.

But wait, there's more! A bit, anyway. In late fall you have one last chance to put some overwintering crops in the ground where those latest-of-the-late summer and fall veggies have finally come out.

Bulbing alliums will slumber for a time in your soil during the harshest weather, but they are the first plants that pop out of the ground in the new year and will spice up next summer's dishes. There is still a bit of time for some cover-crop seeds to sprout, especially fava beans, which also can be sown as a late-spring edible crop.

Tuck the winter vegetables into a cozy bed of thick mulch for the cold season, and similarly mulch your unplanted garden beds for winter protection. Soil temperatures will be back in the 40s by this time, slowing down growth in all but the hardiest vegetable. Set up your sturdiest season-extending devices to protect tender herbs or potted plants, making sure to situate them with a clear path to the low winter sun.

Winter (Late November to Mid-February)

The only planting that happens during the dark and rainy maritime Northwest winter months is

Save Your Own Seeds

Another great way to make gardening more self-sufficient is to save your own seeds. For many vegetables, it takes less effort than you'd expect, and it is a rewarding way to maintain a consistent supply and share seeds of your favorite varieties.

You may save seeds from open-pollinated varieties, which are heirlooms or stable, naturally hybridized plants—not F1 hybrids or patented, genetically modified varieties. Look for the words *open-pollinated* or *heirloom* on the seed packet label.

Dry method: For peas, beans, and crops that form seed heads, such as salad greens, saving seeds is mostly a matter of gathering them up. Let them fully dry in their pods or seed heads, storing them in paper bags in a dry location before shelling them and sorting the seed from the chaff. Some vegetables, such as lettuce, are biennial, going to seed only in their second season, so you have to pay attention to timing. Or you may be challenged by weather; if rain threatens to soak the seed heads, you might have to cover them with paper bags or cut the plant and hang it in a protected location to finish drying.

Wet method: For tomatoes, peppers, and squashes, you must remove the seeds from the pulp, which is a bit messier and involves a different drying regimen. Tomato seeds can be stripped of most of their pulp and put in a jar with water for a few days, agitating it to get the rest of the gel-like covering to release from the seeds. Drain, rinse, and dry on paper plates. Other fruit with internal seeds may require only a good rinse before the seeds can be laid out to dry.

Once you have saved the seeds, proper labeling and storage are crucial. Label the plant, its variety, and the harvest date and store the seeds in paper sleeves or enclosed jars in a dark, dry, cool environment. Monitor regularly and remove any mildewed seed.

Seed life for some vegetables is as short as one year, but some can last many years if stored properly. The average life of seeds is three years.

Seed saving for some vegetables is more challenging, and there are many tricks and techniques to learn. For the best advice, consult *Seed to Seed* by Suzanne Ashworth (see the Resources at the end of this book).

Beets are a winter garden staple.

in your mind as you ponder what went well this year and plan for the next. I find myself pulling back the season extenders on a nice day just to see how everything is faring and check the soil temperature, which often hovers in the mid-30s and can drop lower for a couple of weeks if a cold snap materializes. If unseasonably cold weather threatens, blanket your winter plants with a double cover of season-extension fabrics under their sturdier cloche or cold-frame homes. Covered plants still need watering, but it is best done with tepid water and not very often.

Celebrate the new year by cracking open the garden seed catalogs and reviewing your stored supplies. I often host a seed-ordering party around this time, when we share a potluck of garden-themed dishes with friends and collectively order seeds but also rave about our best successes and decry varieties that did not produce as advertised. By the time the seed orders are placed, it is early spring: time to begin the cycle again.

Before I even start to see the soil warming up, I can picture the garden bursting with plants again.

With every snip of the stem on my winter vegetables, their quantity shrinks but my anticipation builds. The mental image of another gardening year spurs me to get out the seed boxes and start sowing. I watch the calendar and start an inner debate: even though the soil is too cold for outdoor planting, I can still get going by sowing some things indoors.

WHAT TO PLANT WHEN

As my indoor seed-starting begins, it helps to consider the needs of different vegetables. One way is to think about whether they're cool-season or warm-season crops, and the other way is to consider how they grow and whether they're easy to transplant.

Cool-Season or Warm-Season

The estimable Rosalind Creasy, author of *Edible Landscaping,* told a packed house at the 2012 Northwest Flower and Garden Show how to distinguish between a warm-season and a cool-season vegetable: "If you eat the fruit or the seed, it is a warm-season vegetable," she said. "If you eat the leaf, flower bud, or tuber, it prefers cool conditions."

Apply that simple rule, and your planning will be a lot easier. Tomato, fruit; bean, seed: warm-season vegetables. Spinach, leaf; turnip, tuber (well, root, but in this analogy, tubers and roots are similar): happier in cooler conditions. There are exceptions, of course, and she mentioned a couple. Sweet potatoes need heat, even though they're a tuber, and peas (though we eat the seed) set even in cool weather.

Easy or Hard to Transplant

How soon you can start a crop also depends upon whether it can be started indoors and transplanted out. Root crops, generally, are started in their place in the garden, from seed. Thankfully, most roots or tubers fall into the cool-season category and are well suited to year-round growing in the maritime Northwest. Squashes and melons, because they have delicate roots, are best started in the garden, too, although some people start them in pots, which can be done with the right type of pot and very careful handling. Everything else can easily be transplanted.

A Yearly Order of Plantings

Here is an outline of a yearly order of plantings for our region, with a couple of other useful categories for the year-round gardener:

Cool-season crops start off the sowing season in early spring. These vegetables will grow in—or at least tolerate—cooler garden temperatures. Realize that any plants you start indoors in late winter will need to battle "the longest spring on record," which is how I describe the first half of the year in our maritime Northwest to newcomers.

Long-season crops can also be sown in early spring—ones such as leeks that grow through the summer and fall and get harvested in early winter.

Hot-season crops can be sown in midspring. If you get your hot-season vegetables started too early, they will need to spend too much time indoors in the pots before it warms up enough to get them in the soil. By midspring, as your cool-season crops are just about ready to go into their beds, starting the hot crops gives them enough time to size up so you can plant them out when the weather becomes reliably warm.

Root crops, which can be planted from early spring through early fall, are best sown directly into the ground, because it is difficult for the taproot of such a vegetable to be disturbed by transplanting; if it does survive the move, it takes much time and energy to recover and connect with its new home. If you want to get an earlier start with root crops, you must use season-extending techniques over your garden bed, warming and drying the soil and making it ready for those beets and carrots to take the plunge.

Fall and winter crops get started in midsummer; they are more difficult to grow in flats than in their eventual location in the garden, although it can be done with extra diligence about watering during their crucial sprouting and seedling stages. And even though you may think it's easier to just plant the seeds directly into the garden, there are good reasons to start them in flats.

In seed flats, you can get the seedlings started before the beds are cleared of their current crops, and for fall and winter vegetables, the proper timing is key to success. I often start them in flats simply because the garden is full to bursting, and I can't very well rip out producing plants just because I want to plan for the next season. Monitor the summer-sprouting seeds to keep the flats moist until the seedlings emerge, then protect the tender shoots from any bouts of harsh hot weather by locating the flats in a cool spot or covering them with shade cloth during a hot spell.

If you would rather not start things in pots, there are a couple of ways to grow your fall and winter seedlings in the garden. The first is a nursery bed. Simply set aside a space specifically for the seedlings, knowing that you will dig them up and transplant them as space becomes available. Prevent the soil in this bed from drying out too fast by shielding it with a floating row cover.

In some cases, you can sprinkle the seeds for your next crop underneath the leaves of the existing crop and let them get started in potentially cooler, damper conditions. Or, with crop rotation, you can plan ahead so that your garden beds for fall and winter vegetables are coming open just when you need to sow. Those techniques are addressed in detail next.

SUCCESSFUL SUCCESSION PLANTING

Another way to maximize the available soil nutrients is through succession planting, a technique that offers a few other key benefits to year-round growers.

Diversity offers strength—to our bodies, our plants, our overall ecosystem. If we ate only one type of food all the time, even if it were a very healthy food, that lack of diversity in our diets would take its toll. In the ecosystem we create in the garden, lack of diversity would deplete the soil

Quick growing lettuce interplanted with onions will be harvested before the onion bulbs form.

GROWING IN SEVEN SEASONS

From sowing to harvest, it's important to practice proper timing for vegetables grown in the cool-season garden. Here is a guide using my seven miniseasons. Remember to adjust the dates due to local gardening practices and your microclimate.

SEASON	SOW INDOORS	PLANT OUTDOORS WITH SEASON EXTENSION*	PLANT OUTDOORS	HARVEST
Early spring: mid-Feb.– late Mar.	Asian and wild greens, leeks, onions, short-season brassicas	spinach, lettuce, other greens under cloche	peas, fava beans, beets, chard, radish	Asian greens, mustards, chard, collards, sprouting broccoli
Mid-spring: late Mar.– end of May	tomatoes, peppers, basil (then plant out late with season extenders)	late: squashes under floating row cover, cloche, or cold frame	broccoli, peas, onions, parsnips, turnips, cabbage, Brussels sprouts	Asian and wild greens, cabbage, lettuces, peas, sprouting broccoli
Late spring: June– mid-July		wean hot-season crops off their season extenders	fall cabbages, overwintering broccoli, rutabagas, parsnips	spring greens, peas, long-season overwintering veggies (garlic, shallots)
Summer: mid-July– mid-Sept.		tender greens that go under cloche as fall progresses	2nd plantings (fall crops): *July:* brassicas, root crops, Chinese cabbage, chard; *Aug.–Sept.:* salad greens, peas, fall-winter radishes; *late Aug.–early Sept.:* overwintering cabbage, onions, kale, collards, spinach, other Asian greens	summer crops
Early fall: mid-Sept.– mid-Oct.		overwintering peas, carrots, beets, parsnips, lettuces, mustards under floating row cover, cloche, or cold frame		summer crops
Late fall: mid-Oct.– late Nov.			garlic, shallots, fava beans	2nd plantings: brassicas, leeks, greens, peas, root veggies
Winter: late Nov.– mid-Feb.	*Jan.:* lettuce (then transplant to cloche)			chard, mustards, cabbage, Brussels sprouts

* Varies based on your zone, microclimates, and gardening practices

and encourage pests and diseases to run rampant. Creating more diversity through crop rotation, as discussed in chapter 4, feeds the soil, allows us to use less fertilizer, and minimizes the natural forces that can destroy our crops. And keeping the garden full of a variety of plants, sown in succession, helps keep a diversity of food on our table as well as variety in the beds, which helps the entire garden ecosystem thrive.

Tricks of Timing

Perhaps the most vexing challenge for a gardener trying to keep production going year-round is, well, how to keep production going year-round.

"Timing is everything," writes Doug Oster, a nationally syndicated Pittsburgh garden columnist. "One trick I use is to throw lettuce seeds around my tomato plants midsummer," he says in *The Heirloom Gardener*. "They enjoy some shade from the tomatoes. When the season ends for the tomatoes, the lettuce will happily take over after I wrestle out the sprawling vines."

In warm, humid Pittsburgh, Pennsylvania, Doug's summer climate is quite a bit different from ours. But I've tried his underplanting technique with a cover crop, wanting it to sprout while I'm still ripening those last few tomatoes, and it has worked well for me. I prune my tomatoes up off the soil to a foot or so for air circulation, which also provides plenty of room for seedlings. In our maritime climate, dense foliage or other plants too close to the tomato's stem provide ripe conditions for late blight, a fungal disease promoted by the presence of moisture on the tomato plant. If you can keep the other plant's seedlings away from the tomato's stem, and make sure they have adequate water, that is a useful technique.

Doug's gardening experiences are described in books, in the *Pittsburgh Post-Gazette*, on radio, and on television. "To extend the season into winter, I'll sow one last crop of lettuce a few weeks before the expected last frost and cover the area with a floating row cover—that keeps the lettuce cozy all the way into winter," he writes. "The last couple years I've harvested on Christmas Eve." Kudos to him, battling real winter to keep his garden in production.

What's good for Pittsburgh—combining crop rotation and succession planting—would be great for Portland, Oregon. The Pittsburgher also focuses on his next planting: "I'm always looking ahead to my fall crop, and that doesn't mean just greens," Doug writes. "When garlic is harvested in July, bush beans are planted. When a second or third crop of lettuce is done"—and he grows eight crops of the salad staple—"it's replaced with a cole crop like broccoli, kohlrabi, or kale. A second crop of peas is started in August to be picked at the end of September." This is my kind of gardener!

A Different Way of Looking at the Garden

In a conversation about succession planting, Doug tells me this technique has redefined his food gardening. "It's a different way to look at the garden, and it just takes a certain mind-set to make it work. I grew up planting everything on Memorial Day and closing the garden down on Labor Day. That's changed to starting on St. Patrick's Day and harvesting at least through Christmas, sometimes overwintering certain tough greens like tatsoi.

"It's allowed me to stretch, growing things that I'd never heard of before—taking a leap of faith and tasting strange things for the first time. Since I'll eat just about anything, it never seems to be a problem as I discover another fresh garden treat," he says.

"Embracing succession planting might seem like more work, but the harvests are well worth

Recycled materials, like pruned branches and bent bamboo, create an inspirational arbor.

it, and it's exciting to be picking before most gardeners have started planting and well after most gardens are put to bed."

He states the feeling so politely, but if he's like me, there's a bit of triumph in that excitement, too. Since the days of Thomas Jefferson's pea contest and up to the tomato wars held by the uncharacteristically competitive residents in Garrison Keillor's fictitious hometown of Lake Woebegon, we gardeners have always enjoyed a friendly competition. But a one-sided growing contest followed by good-natured gloating is only half the fun. Kidding aside, succession planting is satisfying in many ways: more gardening time, many more vegetables and new varieties to try, better nutrition

on the table throughout the year—for any of those reasons or others more personal to you, it is worth the effort.

Success with succession planting comes from knowing timing tricks for sowing and transplanting, as well as understanding that cool-season crops grow more slowly than their summer versions.

Seven Tricks of Succession Planting

Just like knowing when to start seeds in the spring, we can make many generalities about timing crops to make succession planting work, and while I will detail some of them here, be aware that your unique growing conditions will mean

An attractive bamboo trellis for Japanese cucumbers

that you must adjust these ideas to fit your own garden. Here are seven ways I tackle succession:

Interplant. Sow fall crops between rows of summer crops, if spacing is wide enough. That is similar to Doug's underplanting of fall seeds beneath the canopies of his big tomato plants. I have also sown fall greens under the sprawl of giant summer squash leaves, miniature romaine lettuce heads between rows of onion seedlings, and, conversely, small transplant starts of purple-sprouting broccoli between nearly mature heads of lettuce growing in a grid pattern.

When the older plant is finished producing, don't dig it up, just cut it off at soil level and leave the roots in the ground; otherwise, you could disturb the newer planting. The trick to interplanting

is underground, too: make sure that you aren't robbing pea to pay parsnip, as it were. In other words, you don't want the next crop to pull necessary fertilizer or soil nutrients from the existing crop. Experiment with that in your plot, armed with your soil test and an understanding of which plants are light versus heavy feeders.

Make more room with trellises. Trellis vining crops such as squash and cucumber to give you more space for interplanting and provide easier access (see Three Popular Trellises in the Appendix).

Sow short rows regularly. I typically sow a foot of beets, then when they've gotten their first set of true leaves, I sow another foot, and so on. I might do four beet sowings in spring before thinking I will have enough of my favorite vegetable through the summer.

Vary the varieties. One beet might have a fifty-day maturity date, but for another it might be sixty. If you plant them both at the same time, you'll get a bit of an extended beet harvest; if you plant them ten days apart, you'll get an even longer one. A bonus: you also get variety on the table.

Plant seeds *and* starts. Nip on down to the corner nursery and buy a six-pack of broccoli starts that might be 4 inches tall. While you're there, buy a packet of broccoli seeds as well, then go home and plant out both seeds and starts in a grid that meets their ultimate spacing needs. The starts will feed you first, and just as they start to bolt, the seeded plants will be heading up.

This technique does not work for all plants, of course. Most root crops should only be started from seed. Also, the timing for that crop of seeds must be right; if you tried it late in the optimum sowing period for broccoli, you might find it difficult to bring the seeded crop of broccoli to a productive maturity.

Clear and claim. Be a bit ruthless about deciding the end of productivity for a crop, and when it's straggling along with just a bit more food on it, clear it out and claim the space for the next crop. Add fertilizer and drop fall or winter seedlings into that spot. If you plan for this at the beginning of the year (I like to draw out a map of my beds and track the plantings from season to season), you will be more likely to have the seeds ready or the plants started.

Nurse things along. Always have a nursery bed going, so that you'll have an array of choices to take advantage of some free space. Perhaps you have one summer crop that just doesn't take, or the plants get hit hard by pests. If you can solve the cultural problem and know the bed could handle another crop, survey the choices from your nursery bed, pluck out a few plants, and start fresh.

Succession planting provides a longer harvest.

Or perhaps those Brussels sprouts seeds just didn't make it, and now you have only half a bed of sprouts and it's late July. Pull some overwintering cabbages from your nursery bed, and you can easily add variety to your brassica bed.

What a Succession Plan Looks Like

Here's an example of one plan:

- **Midspring:** In late May I sow some long-season cabbages in a seed flat to have them ready for transplanting in a month.
- **Late spring:** I always harvest my garlic at the end of June, so I plan for that to be my overwintering cabbage bed.
- **Interplanting:** When I put those cabbage seedlings in the former garlic bed, I also sow some leaf-lettuce seeds.
- **Backup plan:** If I want to hedge my bets on the cabbage, I also choose one with a bit shorter season and direct-sow it in this bed as well or purchase some starts to add to the mix.
- **Next midspring:** Once I begin harvesting the first of the overwintered cabbages, I plant another row of lettuce between them.
- **Next summer:** When the greens are waning in midsummer, I can sow a cover crop and essentially let this bed rest for a season, or I can add lime and compost and put in some fall salad greens or overwintering carrots.

SLOWER GROWING RATES IN COOL SEASONS

Another concept to add to the calculations for year-round production is the idea that growing crops in the cool seasons is a slower prospect than in the summer. The plants may leap out of the soil in the spring, but you might not get that great leaping start with fall plantings. These different growth rates have to do with day length (available hours for photosynthesis) and warmth (number of hours above a plant's minimum growing rate).

Studying Growth Rates

A few years ago, researcher Carol Miles and a team from Washington State University ran tests on growing winter lettuces in western Washington—at WSU's trial gardens in Vancouver, near the Oregon state line—and their results on growth rates, from transplanting to maturity dates, were fascinating. In the winter of 2004–5, for instance, they tended nearly three dozen varieties of lettuce (butterhead, loose-leaf, romaine, and more) in different growing environments. Part of the trial took place in large hoop houses, the size that a person can walk upright in, not the small ones we use in backyard gardens. They also planted some in a cloche, but again, not the type we use at home. Their cloche was a wire tunnel, but it was covered with a heavy-fabric floating row cover rather than plastic. They hand-watered the hoop-house plants, but the cloche received natural watering, as the rain enters right through the fabric covering. Although their goal was to study conditions for commercial market growing, home gardeners can learn from their results, too.

They performed three plantings in the fall—two in the hoop houses, on September 30 and October 21, and one in the cloche, also on October 21. They also performed one spring planting, on March 3, in one of the hoop houses. They found the seedlings planted in the fall were ready for transplanting in two months, but the spring-planted seedlings were able to be transplanted in six weeks.

What's more, their tracking of harvest dates revealed a surprising range—and amazing length—of the growing season. Seed catalogs list dozens of lettuces with varying days to maturity that range from about 35 to 75. Many of them are in the 45- to 55-day range. For the spring planting in Miles's tests, the average days to maturity was 42, about what you'd expect from the seed-packet instructions. But the fall-started varieties took much longer, even in the large hoop houses. In one, the average was 97 days, and in the other it was 112 days (the two hoop houses were different styles). Outdoors in the fabric-covered cloche, the lettuce took an average of 130 days to come to maturity. "Growth in a field cloche," write the researchers, "is significantly slower (30 days) than in a hoop house during the coldest months." But even in the hoop houses, the length of time to grow your winter salad more than doubles.

Extending Growing Rates at Home

In my unscientific home tests over the years, I have seen similar results. For instance, in 2011 I seeded lettuce on October 15, which is a couple of weeks later than my normal cutoff date, but I was doing it under a plastic-covered hoop-house cloche and wanted to push the envelope. Both Red Oak Leaf and Marvel of Four Seasons germinated by the end of October, and sturdy little plants, perhaps an inch tall with two to three sets of leaves, were crowding their rows by mid-November. At that point, I covered the plants with a layer of floating row cover and tucked them in under the cloche, so they had two layers of protection. A mid-January storm gave us nearly a week of temperatures in the high 20s and blanketed the cloche with snow for a few days, but our weather was back to its seasonal normal (40°F by day, mid-30s by night) by the end of the month.

When I uncovered the cloche and pulled away the floating row cover on February 5, I found healthy plants with leaves nearly 3 inches long, allowing the first cutting at 110 days. In mid-February, I took the floating row cover away and let the lettuce grow freely under the plastic cloche. In fact, I started more lettuce, spinach, and carrots in the remaining cloche space. The plants continued to produce well into the spring, offering abundant salad volume by late March. By early April, I rolled up the ends of the cloche to allow air to flow freely through it, leaving the covering over the top to control the moisture.

In real estate, it is always said that "you can change the house, but you can't change the location," and that is true in the garden as well. To paraphrase that old slogan, you can change the microclimate, but you can't move the sun.

Season extension, which I used to good effect on those winter lettuces, is discussed in chapters 7 and 8. It is the way to change the microclimate and combat one of those limitations on growing. If, early in the year, you can provide enough warmth for plant growth to begin, you'll have more time for succession planting. Similarly, if you can guarantee (through season extension) that warmth in fall will extend past the date when outdoor temperatures dip below those needed for plant growth, you can do as I did with the lettuce and sow fall and winter crops that take a little longer season.

Each year, your needs for season extension will probably be a little different. If we have a warm spring, you can pull those season-extending devices off the bed earlier or begin some crops without even using them. If a cold snap happens much earlier in fall than expected, you may lose an unprotected bed of tender fall greens if you aren't paying attention. I keep an eye on the weather forecast and my own conditions, and I often find myself running out to the garden at the last minute to toss a protective covering over a crop when a frost seems imminent or when an unexpected deluge threatens to drown a bed or trigger rot.

THE "DAYS TO MATURITY" FACTOR

Along with watching the weather, planning your succession planting in a perpetual garden journal, and studying the needs of each crop, you can apply a couple of formulas to help identify proper calendar dates for sowing and succession planting.

Maturity Date from Seed or Transplant

To start with, understand how to work from a plant's maturity date to find the planting date. "Days to maturity" is itself a relative term. For most crops, that number of days listed on the seed packet is from the date of sowing the seed outdoors.

For a few crops, though, the date indicates days from *transplanting* to maturity. That is especially true of hot-season crops such as peppers and tomatoes, and this fact may or may not be indicated in the seed catalog or on the packet. Large members of the *Brassica* genus (broccoli, Brussels sprouts, cabbage, and cauliflower) are the only cool-season crops I'm aware of that are typically transplanted and so would be likely to have their days to maturity listed as transplant dates. Many other cool-season crops can be started in pots and transplanted, but calculate maturity dates as you would if sowing the seed.

Maturity Date to Start or End of Harvest Period

A second consideration about the number of days to maturity is that it may indicate only the *beginning* of a harvest that may last for quite some time. If a butterhead lettuce variety is listed at forty-eight days to maturity, you may be snipping leaves from its loosely forming head as early as thirty-five days or as long as sixty days. Even when a cool-season crop such as cabbage or carrots is mature, it may be fine staying in the garden for another week or even a more couple months if conditions are right.

Even though we are concentrating on cool-season vegetables, our planning needs to consider the maturity date and harvest period of warm-season vegetables too, because that calculation tells us when the crop will be done and we can continue with succession planting. A pepper might take sixty days from transplanting to pro-duce its first ripe green fruit but fifteen more days to produce any red peppers. After the first red

pepper, the plant will still grow and ripen peppers for weeks, and you can pick them at the stage of ripeness and hotness that you desire.

Calculating the Maturity Date

To get fall and winter crops started at the right time, it is especially important to calculate the maturity date. Here are a couple of rules of thumb:

- **Add a "fall factor."** Add ten to fourteen days to the maturity number because of lower light or shorter days, hence fewer hours in the day for photosynthesis. In the fall, a sixty-day carrot might take seventy to seventy-four days.

Another Route: Leave It to the Professionals!

The flier read, "Take the guesswork out of veg-etable gardening with well-planned succession of plant starts." Hmm, I thought. This could be the subtitle for my book. Instead, it was a colorful promotion from Cascadian Edible Landscapes, an urban gardening service in Seattle whose slogan is "Eat Your Yard."

I knew that Michael Seliga and his team had been setting up and tending vegetable gardens for a few years, specializing in getting gardens to urban people who don't quite have the time to do it all themselves. But this was something different. Instead of offering their services, they were offering plants.

Seliga sprouted Community Supported Plant Starts (CSPS) as "a community sup-ported agriculture (CSA) program for edible plant starts." Borrowing from the CSA model, Cascadian signs people up for year-round deliveries of vegetable starts, which are sea-sonally appropriate and designed to keep the garden producing all year. Subscribers get

plant deliveries in April, June, August, and September, and in between they get the com-pany's newsletter with crop-tending advice.

"It's a garden in a box," he tells me. "We're trying to get people good-quality plant starts and some education on growing year-round." A small subscription is one flat with about ten plants per season, up to fifteen in the summer. Driven by customer demand, by the program's fourth year it offered more than forty choic-es. Brussels sprouts are surprisingly popular, along with a colorful kale mix that's all planted together. In 2011, a customer survey showed that 88 percent of subscribers were growing more food than in the past.

The program also has evolved to build on the "community" aspect, including workshops and a seed-saving element, and Cascadian even partnered with students at two schools in 2012 to use the program as a fund-raiser. "Instead of selling chocolate bars," Seliga says, "they're selling plants!"

• **Consider the harvest period.** You may be able to get a short-maturing lettuce to its maturity date before the winter rains or first frosts, but are you willing to erect protection over the crop to keep it feeding you during its whole two- to four-week harvest period? Many gardeners can remember tending a nice crop right up to its maturity date, but their anticipation for many meals from it was dashed by an overnight frost that left behind wilted or slimy plants, formerly food but now simply compost.

An Example of a Maturity Date Calculation

To calculate your fall plantings, follow this four-step process: (1) Start with your first frost date as a general guideline. (2) Working backward, count the number of days or weeks of the expected harvest period. (3) Then count back the number of days to maturity listed for the variety you're considering. (4) Add a fall factor. These steps should give you your planting date. For instance, let's try this with a fall broccoli listed at seventy days:

1. Assume my first frost date in Seattle is October 26 (low probability, but I am being cautious).
2. My experience is that I get about a ten-day harvest period for this crop, so I count backward to October 16 for the start of my harvest period.
3. Then I count backward seventy days to August 7 for my days to maturity—but remember for this crop, the maturity date is calculated from transplanting. It typically takes twenty days in midsummer to get my broccoli sprouted and up to transplant size (whether I start it in a flat or a nursery bed), because I presprout the seeds indoors before sowing. So I count backward another twenty days to July 18.
4. Broccoli grows pretty consistently in my microclimate, even if there's cool fall weather, so I add

ten more days as a moderate fall factor. That brings me to July 8 for a sowing date. Northwest seed companies typically advise planting broccoli up until July 15, so my timing should be just fine. If I had chosen a broccoli with more days to maturity, it might not have worked. Often it's best to choose the shorter season varieties for fall harvests.

The Succession Planting Factor

One more useful element to this calculation takes into account succession planting. In step 3 above, I found that August 7 would be my date to begin calculating days to maturity, and in this case it would also be my transplant date. I can use that transplant date when I plan my garden to help me decide where to put a fall broccoli crop and what else will go in that bed this year.

To decide where the broccoli will go, I need to determine what plants likely will be at the end of their harvest period and ready to be pulled out by that date, as well as what would be appropriate for proper crop rotation, as covered in chapter 4.

Because early August is the middle of my prime summer growing season, I know I won't be putting the fall broccoli in any of those spots—it will have to be a bed planted with overwintered, spring-sown, or very short-season crops. Garlic and peas will have been gone for a month or so, and I can usually find a crop of lettuce or other greens ready to be rotated out, so that's where the broccoli will end up.

Finally, it helps to think ahead, too. What will I do with this bed when I pull the broccoli? There's not much that can be planted at the end of October, but there are a few things. That is the time to plant garlic and shallots, which will overwinter and be dug in early summer. Fava beans can be put in, to overwinter for spring eating or as a cover crop, and you might catch the end of the sowing period for small-grain cover crops.

By charting out this calculation for each crop you'd like to grow each year, you can see a pattern of which ones could be paired in the same bed for succession planting, thereby bringing full cycle your plan to use your garden year-round, taking in all the considerations of weather conditions, soil needs, proper growing periods for plants, and, most important, your goal of eating food from your garden through the seasons.

COOL-SEASON KEYS TO EXPANDING YOUR SEASONAL SENSIBILITY

- Rethink four seasons to seven miniseasons for more detailed planning.
- Differentiate cool-season from warm-season crops.
- Keep a rotational plan per bed.
- Maintain a nursery bed for the next crop in succession.
- Use space more effectively with trellising and interplanting.
- Add winter grow rates and a fall factor to accurately plan harvests.

7

Taking Easy Steps to Extend the Growing Season

Rained steadily today.
Daylight hours are now shorter than working hours.
Chill wind in the air—you can really feel winter coming.
Checked the soil temperature, and it's hovering at 40°F.

If these are your thoughts or garden journal entries during late fall and winter, I sympathize. I also commend you. The pat on the back comes because you are making note of the weather, which is a favorite spectator sport of food gardeners. But my empathetic hug comes for the same reason. We seem to live and die—and our vegetables literally do—by the forecast.

Never have I seen such furrowed brows or quizzical looks as when gardeners in cool climates talk about the weather. We are concerned constantly about the temperature, rainfall, and day length. In the spring we urge on those lengthening days and warming nights, and in the summer we glory over early sunrises and wax poetic about the warmth on our stooped backs. But in autumn our concerns begin to grow in reverse proportion to nighttime temperatures—every five-degree drop results in another nervous tic. We fuss over the inglorious end to summer's abundance, debating how long to keep heat-loving crops in the ground, just to ripen a few more tomatoes or get one more summer squash to size up. Summer-focused gardeners reluctantly discuss plans for "putting the garden to bed."

Cool-season gardeners, though, get a break from all that late-summer angst, because we are one with the weather: Acting rather than reacting. Moving forward rather than scaling back. Conquering rather than relinquishing! OK, maybe that last one is a bit of a stretch. Mother nature, after all, wields a bigger hammer with all her climate changes than we mere humans can shoulder. However, we can step into that chill wind, wipe the mist from our faces, and look to the sky for signs of a break in the clouds, because we have a shield to hold up against all that: it's six mil thick and is called season extension.

Many tools, techniques, and gardening practices can be called season extension, and I hope when you finish reading that you will feel comfortable trying at least some of them. We already have explored some in earlier chapters: finding the best site for your garden is vitally important, as is building the soil and maintaining its fertility. The techniques of crop rotation, succession planting, pruning, and trellising also help a cool-climate gardener extend the growing season on both ends.

But specific season-extending techniques are targeted to the practice of growing food year-round, versus just getting the most out of summer. To begin with, my definition of season extension has a few criteria. With season extension, you can:

- Start growing food earlier in the spring.
- Get your vegetables to ripen earlier, which means you can harvest earlier.
- Enhance weather conditions with special devices and techniques.
- Grow many fall and winter crops.

This chapter covers basic season-extension efforts, including easy steps with little or no extra equipment and midlevel tactics requiring a bit of construction ability and specialized gardening knowledge. The next chapter looks at advanced practices requiring construction expertise (or at least some tools and the willingness to experiment) and bigger devices for large-scale production. The Appendix offers do-it-yourself plans for selected season-extension building projects.

A corollary to these three levels of season-extending techniques relates to your time commitment, which ranges from taking extra steps during the spring planting season to starting seeds indoors to building raised beds. Tending to season-extension tasks weekly throughout the year is an advanced approach covered in the next chapter.

Once you have tried these season-extending techniques—and you have the materials on hand—experiment with the devices in your garden.

Because I've learned much from other gardeners over the years and I regularly see new ways people use season extension, I know I'm only just scratching the surface of creative methods to protect crops for year-round growing. One of these days, I want to be invited into your garden to see your unique take on these ideas!

BASIC SEASON-EXTENSION EFFORTS

One of the simplest ways to practice season extension is to warm the soil before spring plantings by using a plastic cover. Another easy step is to keep the seedbed a bit cozier by laying down a permeable fabric "blanket" after sowing. These methods do not require construction expertise or a great amount of specialized knowledge.

Warm Up the Garden by Solarizing the Soil

If you do nothing else before you start gardening this spring, head out to the garden when the sun is shining and cover the soil in plastic. That is not something to be done indiscriminately, but the step of covering your soil for a time before planting can have significant benefits.

First, it will help your soil dry out a bit sooner during the long, wet kiss that nature bestows on the maritime Northwest landscape, and you will be able to get the early-season seeds or seedlings in the soil.

Second, this process—which is sometimes called solarizing the soil—will warm up the garden bed. As it warms, the worms and other soil organisms also increase in number and activity. You need them to help transport nutrients to the plant roots, aerate the soil, and fight off soil-borne pests and diseases that could harm your plants.

Third, if you use black plastic, it can kill some of the weeds that overwintered in the bed, which will make your garden prep easier.

Convinced? Then here's what to do: use a heavy black or clear plastic sheeting, four or six mil thick. That thickness of plastic will hold up under repeated uses in the garden, and the clear material also can be used as a cloche covering. Roll it out to the size of your garden bed and cut off the excess. Hold it down securely with rocks, boards, or anything that will prevent it from being pulled up by the wind. You can even dig a shallow trench along each edge of the bed, tuck the plastic into the trench, and cover it over, thereby using the soil to hold down the sheeting.

Sow lettuce seeds under clear plastic when the soil temperature reaches 50°F, Joyce McClellan, owner of Ornamental Edibles in San Jose, California, advises in a gardening column for Bay Area gardeners. When she did that, soil temperatures quickly rose to 70°F, causing lettuce to sprout in three days. I have seen very quick sprouting in seed trays with heat mats that raised the soil to that temperature, so I can believe it. But be very vigilant with this technique, because the plastic must come off immediately after the tender green shoots hit the light, or the solarizing effect will quickly cook them.

A couple of other cautions about solarizing with plastic: Do this just for the weeks before you're planting; don't leave it on all winter. Garden soil covered for long periods of time loses its soil food web of beneficial microorganisms, and that takes a long time to rebuild when you start gardening in it again. A better solution for the whole winter on a bed you're not using is to plant a cover crop, which helps build soil and protect the ground from compaction and nutrient leaching during winter rains.

Also, don't expect this treatment to kill all the weeds. The black plastic treatment might kill the very small ones that are just sprouting. Larger weeds, or those with runner-type roots such as bindweed, will rejuvenate once the plastic is removed. Using clear plastic as a cover can actually have the opposite results with weeds, creating a greenhouse effect that causes the weed seeds to sprout. That is not a bad problem, because you can just scrape off the young weeds after removing the plastic.

One final caution is to make sure the plastic cover does not cause a problem elsewhere in the yard. The impervious surface will send rainwater running off, and if the garden slopes toward a sensitive area, you could have problems, such as water in your basement. Try to picture the unintended consequences that could arise and take steps to avoid them.

Eventually, if you follow many of the other suggestions in this book, you won't have much open soil in your garden to treat this way in the spring, because you'll be using most of your bed space year-round. But it's a good way to get your spring gardening under way earlier.

What Is a "Mil"?

When you shop for plastic sheeting, you will see the thickness expressed as two mil, four mil, six mil, et cetera. Thinner products are just called "painter's plastic" or "dropcloth," so if they don't express their thickness in mils, they are probably too thin to use in the garden.

A mil is not, as you might think, a shortened version of "millimeter." Instead, it expresses thickness in increments of one-thousandths of an inch. So two-mil plastic is 0.002 inch thick, and ten-mil is 0.010 inch thick. For comparison, a sheet of standard copier paper is about four mil thick.

FLOATING ROW COVERS

Lightweight "garden fleece" helps warm the soil and keep out bugs, but lets air, light, and water through.

PRODUCT	TYPE OF MATERIAL	WIDTH	WEIGHT/ SQ. YD.	LIGHT TRANS- MISSION	FROST PROTEC- TION	COST PER LENGTH
Floating Cover (Reemay) by A. M. Leonard	Spun-bonded polyester	67 in.	0.6 oz.	69%	*	20 ft. $10.95; 100 ft. $29.95
Germination and Insect Blanket by A. M. Leonard	*	6 ft.	0.5 oz.	85%	*	250 ft. $28.49
Summerweight Fabric	Feather-weight polypropylene	6 ft.	0.5 oz.	85%	28°F	20 ft. $7.95; 50 ft. $12.95
All-Purpose Garden Fabric	Point-bonded polypropylene	6 ft.; 12 ft.	0.9 oz.	70%	28°F	6 ft. x 20 ft. $9.95; 6 ft. x 50 ft. $18.95; 12 ft. x 20 ft. $16.95
Agribon+ AG-15 Insect Barrier	Spun-bonded polypropylene	118 in.	0.45 oz.	90%	28°F	50 ft. $21.95
Agribon+ AG-19 Floating Row Cover	Spun-bonded polypropylene	83 in.; 10 ft.	0.55 oz.	85%	28°F	83 in. x 50 ft. $21.95; 10 ft. x 50 ft. $27.95
Harvest Guard by Dalen	Spun-bonded polyester	5 ft.	*	*	29°F; 2 layers 26°F	5 ft. x 25 ft. $16; 5 ft. x 50 ft. $28
Frost Protek Plant Cover	Spun-bonded polypropylene	5 ft.	0.9 oz.	70%	26°F	5 ft. x 10 ft. $10.95
Crop Cover	Spun-bonded polypropylene	6 ft.; 12 ft.	1.0 oz.	80%	26°F	6 ft. x 50 ft. $14.95; 6 ft. x 100 ft. $29.95; 12 ft. x 25 ft. $14.95
Insect Mesh Grow Tunnel by Gardman USA	*	15 in.	*	*	*	10 ft. $28
Fleece Grow Tunnel by Gardman USA	*	20 in.	*	*	*	10 ft. $28
Giant Tunnel Cloche by Gardman USA	*	39 in.	*	*	*	6.5 ft. $26
Garden Quilt	Spun-bonded polypropylene	6 ft.; 12 ft.	1.25 oz.	60%	24°F	6 ft. x 20 ft. $12.95; 6 ft. x 50 ft. $21.95; 12 ft. x 20 ft. $19.95
Frost Blanket by A. M. Leonard	*	6 ft.; 12 ft.; 24 ft.	1.5 oz.; 3.0 oz.	50%; 40%	*	Sized by large rolls

*Information not available

Note: Suppliers and prices accurate as of spring 2012; see Resources for contact information.

SUPPLIER	COMMENTS
A. M. Leonard; Amazon	Lightweight
A. M. Leonard	Lightweight; sized by large rolls
Gardener's Supply—exclusive	Lightweight
Gardener's Supply—exclusive	Midweight
Johnny's Seeds; Peaceful Valley	Commercial version also available
Johnny's Seeds; Peaceful Valley	Same as above
Home improvement centers; Amazon	
Charley's Greenhouse	Light green; also comes as "bags," which are pricier
Charley's Greenhouse	
Home improvement centers; Amazon	Preassembled with wire hoop frame, 18 in. tall
Home improvement centers; Amazon	Preassembled with wire hoop frame, 18 in. tall
Home improvement centers; Amazon	Preassembled with wire hoop frame, 24 in. tall
Gardener's Supply—exclusive	Heavyweight crop protection, not for growing
A. M. Leonard; Burpee	Heavyweight crop protection, not for growing

Blanket Plants with Floating Row Cover

Another easy early-season technique that warms and dries the soil a bit but also provides a beneficial effect on seedlings in the soil is to cover your spring bed with floating row cover (FRC).

FRC is generally a light-colored fabric, most often made of spun-bonded (not woven) polypropylene, sold under brand names such as Reemay, Harvest Guard, or Garden Quilt. It is very lightweight, so it won't damage plants that it is covering, even emerging seedlings. (The last brand mentioned is a heavier material mostly used to wrap tender plants when a freeze is expected or for longer winter periods in colder areas.)

The particular qualities of FRC make it very useful to year-round gardeners, especially in the early spring. The fabric allows water and light to get through, but holds in a bit of the heat gained from the sun on a warm day and causes the soil to release its stored heat more slowly at night. I have recorded a consistent increase of one or two degrees in soil on which I've used FRC compared to bare beds in the same conditions.

FRC also holds in moisture, which is great for seedlings. You don't have to water as often or worry about the bed getting too dry on a freakishly warm day while you have seeds sprouting. You can water right through the material, which lies flat against the soil or drapes over the seedlings until it dries out enough to regain its loft.

FRC also makes a great barrier to keep insects away from your seedlings, so the slugs won't chomp down all the lettuce starts and the carrot rust fly can't lay its eggs at the base of the carrot seedlings. It also keeps cats from using your freshly dug bed as their bathroom.

When you "make the bed" with FRC, use a piece that is a couple of square feet larger than the bed size. Secure the edges of the material to

Floating row cover, sometimes called garden fleece, keeps greens cozy.

the edges of the bed as you would do with a plastic cover, and let the excess material float in the center of the bed. That will allow the seedlings to push it up without too much resistance. I've found that burying the edges of the FRC is especially useful for keeping out pests (although any pests already in the bed will stay in there). Burying the edge has a drawback, though, if you need to monitor the progress of the plantings. If that's the case, use long boards to securely anchor the FRC on all sides, paying extra attention to the windward side, because if it flaps in the breeze, it does no good for your soil or your plants.

MIDLEVEL TACTICS TO EXTEND THE GROWING SEASON

A moderately challenging way to practice season extension is to start your vegetable seeds indoors and then plant them out after they've sized up (see chapter 5). Once your seedlings have gotten their great start indoors and are ready to be planted into the garden bed, a whole series of season-extension techniques and devices can help them grow more robustly in a cool climate. Other options at the next level up from basic efforts are to protect crops with small plastic or glass cloches that fit over each plant and to build raised beds for your vegetable garden.

Cloches for Single Plants

To quote film director Billy Wilder, some like it hot, and that goes for plants as well as ingenues. Tomatoes, peppers, eggplant, squashes, and melons all are genetically predisposed to thrive and produce their voluptuous fruit in a warmer climate. If you're a cool-climate gardener, there are still steps you can take to make up for the weather. The easiest method (although not efficient for a large quantity of seedlings or for row crops) is to simply cover each plant with its own little cloche. The word *cloche* is French for "bell," which provides a clue to the first such devices.

Bells

Market gardeners whose task was to feed fresh vegetables to the people of Paris all winter pioneered the use of glass cloches in their fields, and the practice was in wide use in the eighteenth century. That was an intensive effort, because a solid glass bell set on the soil creates a much warmer, more humid environment than plastic does. The common historical image of gardeners tending the cloched plants shows a number of people stooping over the bells and propping them open to keep the veggies from being cooked. Such small cloches are really miniature greenhouses that bring the warmth down to individual plants.

You can still find glass bell cloches, and it would be especially pleasing to come across old ones at antique stores. I know some gardeners who have

Traditional French bell cloche

Recycled plastic bottle cloche

a couple around as useful curiosities. My friend Willi Galloway, a fellow garden writer and stellar kitchen gardener, has a graceful glass cloche she uses as an indoor decoration most of the year but sets out over some seeds in the spring.

More common are plastic or waxed-paper versions of the bell cloche. Clear plastic ones, which come in a few variations on the bell shape, typically have a top vent that can be spun open so you don't have to prop up the base to lower the heat and humidity. They also have a flat lip on the bottom of the bell with holes so you can stake it down and prevent the lightweight cover from blowing away in the wind. These all have to be removed for watering, and the warmth they generate does dry out the soil fairly quickly, so daily monitoring is necessary.

You can get plastic cloches with a coating to combat UV light so they will last longer before the sun's rays break them down. Some are made of polyvinyl chloride (PVC), but others are made

of recycled or recyclable plastics such as polyethylene terephthalate (PET) or polypropylene.

Translucent cloches made of waxed paper, although they let through less light, have some appeal too. They are a more environmentally friendly choice, inexpensive and disposable. Both plastic and waxed-paper cloches can be purchased in a batch, so you'll have enough to cover a row of lettuce, little round mounds protecting one head at a time.

Other "Hot Cap" Styles

You can make bell cloches as your own recycling project, too. Most common ones I've seen are two-liter PET soda or juice bottles and gallon milk jugs. Bottles with screw tops can easily be vented. Strip off their labels, cut off their bottoms, and they're nearly ready for the garden. One more step: cut two 1-inch parallel slits up from the bottom on each side to create two plastic tabs. Bend their edges up and punch holes in them. That will allow you to slip a wire ground staple through each hole and hold the cloche from blowing away.

Look around your home or work for other transparent or lightly translucent plastic that might work as a protection for your seedlings. I've seen people use clear deli containers, although those have to be propped open for venting. The biggest plastic cloche I've seen is a water-cooler jug. Its blue-tinted surface and oversize soda-bottle shape added an interesting sculptural element to the garden, and because of its size, the gardener typically lets the plant get quite big before removing the cloche.

Wall o' Water

One small commercial cloche that improves on the hot cap concept is called the Wall o' Water. Also marketed as Kozy Coat or Season Extender, this plastic contraption is a minigreenhouse that really intensifies the heat on a young hot-season

Connected plastic tubes form a Wall o' Water.

crop. The Wall o' Water is a circle of plastic tubes that are connected vertically, with each tube open at one end. Slip the device upright over a plant, fill the tubes with water, and the tubes lean together in a tepee shape around the plant. You must be careful when erecting this device over a plant to prevent it from slumping and snapping the plant's stem, as well as to keep your garden hose from drowning the plant while you fill the tubes.

To avoid these problems, here's what I do: I place a five-gallon bucket upside down over the plant, making sure the plant is centered under the bucket. Then I slip the empty Wall o' Water over the bucket. If the bucket has a handle, make sure it's not under the edge of the Wall o' Water, because it can be messy to free the handle once the tubes are full of water. Equip the garden hose with a good shut-off valve, and open the hose in short spurts to methodically fill the tubes, taking care not to soak the ground around the device. Fill a few tubes on one side, then go across to the opposite side, continuing until all are three-quarters filled. Then carefully pull the bucket straight up and allow the walls of the device to lean into each other. You can reposition it a bit once it's in place to get the desired tepee shape and amount of opening in the top.

Care must be taken to vent the Wall o' Water on a warm day to avoid burning the plant. Also helpful is a drip irrigation system that can send a tube under the edge of the minigreenhouse and deliver water to the base of the plant. Watering inside the Wall o' Water is difficult, as an overhead sprinkler may not penetrate adequately through the small top opening, and watering individually with a hose or wand is time-consuming and awkward. In addition, overhead watering is not advisable for some plants because getting their leaves and stems wet can lead to rot.

As the plant grows, stake the minigreenhouse open with a piece of bamboo or other support stakes. When the plant has grown well past the top of the tubes, carefully pull the Wall o' Water off over the top of the plant. Do this in the morning so that if you spill some water when removing it, your wet plant will dry during the day. You will need the device on hot crops until you get nighttime temperatures reliably in the high 50s, which doesn't happen in most places in the maritime Northwest until mid-July.

Wall o' Water can be useful on other plants besides the hot summer crops. I've tried it in early spring when sprouting peas, although you can do only a small batch and not a long row. I've also used it to warm and dry the soil and then sprouted lettuce seed under it. For these cool-season crops, the device should not be used for their entire growth period. Stake it open after the plants have two sets of true leaves. When the nighttime temperatures consistently hover in the high 40s, the Wall o' Water is not needed to help cool-season crops continue to grow.

Elevate Your Veggies with a Raised Bed

While hot caps can warm up individual plants, there is a fairly easy way to warm up an entire garden: build a raised bed. It will help dry and warm the soil earlier in the spring, so you can get those peas vining while your neighbor's soil is still warming up. Along with drier, warmer soil, a raised bed may be easier to work, will allow you to control the type and quality of soil, and can define the vegetable garden in a way that is both protective and attractive. And if you put hot caps on your plants on top of the raised bed, you get double the effect!

Got an old pickup truck sitting around not in use? How about loading up its back end with soil for the ultimate raised bed? That's what the folks at the Urban Farm Company did as an entertaining display for the 2010 Northwest Flower and Garden Show in Seattle.

But they took the concept a couple of steps further: They removed the hood, pulled the engine, and filled that compartment with soil and food, too, even planting a tree (which, thinking of the shade and root system, might have been going a bit too far). Not content to stop there, they also had chickens roosting and laying in the cab. It was an impressive recycling project, to be sure, and an award-winning garden show display.

To take a more pedestrian approach to gardening—and avoid the rusting-metal contamination of your garden soil—consider building a raised bed from more conventional materials, such as:

- Wood planks and posts
- Composite lumber
- Stackable pavers or bricks
- Flat chunks of broken concrete sidewalks (which I've recently heard referred to as "urbanite")
- Rust-inhibiting metals (galvanized or weathering steel, in sheets or containers)

You also can just mound the soil up so that it's permanently higher than the ground around it. If using materials, stack or prop them up to define the edge of your garden. Make sure they're sturdy so that if you sit or stand on them, they won't topple.

Raised beds can be as low as 6 inches or as high as 4 feet; the higher ones are especially useful for gardeners with limited mobility. The height is determined by cost, available materials, and personal comfort. You might need professional engineering or construction help to make sure taller raised beds are safe and secure.

Because the bed will get sunlight on its sides as well as the top, it will warm and dry a bit earlier in the spring. Also, because you can fill it with a special vegetable-garden soil mix, it will perhaps have better drainage than your native garden soil, which again means you can work it earlier in the spring.

Whether you stack up some bricks or broken concrete, screw together some wood or plastic lumber, or take out a home-improvement loan to haul in sheet steel, a raised bed in the garden offers significant benefits to your year-round growing, and it is the base upon which all other season-extension techniques can be layered. Here are some notes on each type of material for raised beds.

Wood

Using planks or stacked 4-by-4-inch lumber— a natural, renewable material—as your raised bed is a fine choice. If the raised bed is made with lumber, you can attach pieces that will support your cloche or cold frame as well, so it can do double duty as a season extender.

A wood garden bed does not have to be expensive, as reclaimed, recycled lumber is now readily available at stores specializing in salvaged building products or even from neighboring construction sites, whose workers will stack their scrap lumber on the curb with a sign that uses the favorite word of the frugal gardener: "Free!" You can also use downed logs or even smaller trunks and

Raised beds can be made of many materials.

branches, stacked up loosely and staked to hold them together.

Treated wood? Many gardeners stay away from using treated lumber, and certainly it is wise to avoid the old types of treated wood, such as creosote-soaked railroad timbers or pressure-treated wood with chromated copper arsenate (CCA). Oh, boy, arsenic! That's the last thing you want to introduce to your garden, especially the vegetable bed. According to Linda Chalker-Scott, a Washington State University Extension urban horticulturist and associate professor, there is plentiful evidence in scientific tests that chromium and arsenic do leach out of the old-formula treated wood. She addresses the issue in her excellent book *The Informed Gardener* and notes research showing that those chemicals also are taken up into the edible parts of many vegetables. Resolve not to use that kind of wood, or just get rid of it.

If you inherit a bed with those types of wood in place and cannot remove it, dig a trench next to the offensive wood and drop a heavy plastic barrier between the wood and your soil—a forty-mil-thick sheet, the type used to contain bamboo rhizomes, would provide a good barrier. Have the soil tested for arsenic and chromium. Even consider an entire plastic liner for your raised bed, with holes poked in the bottom for drainage and filled with new, uncontaminated soil.

The current types of treated wood are much less worrisome. Chalker-Scott recommends using many other types of materials for raised beds, as discussed here, but notes that pressure-treated wood sold today is less toxic, treated with chemicals such as copper and boron, which are acceptable alternatives.

Although there are a number of treated woods, the two common types you might see use alkaline copper quarternary (ACQ) or copper azole (CA), of which there are a few generations, labeled A, B, and C. Which one is available in your area might be determined by geography and the mill's choice. On the West Coast, the common species of timber used for treated lumber are coastal Douglas fir and western hemlock. These both lend themselves to the CA treatment. In other areas of the United States where southern pine is more available, you might see more ACQ.

Other solutions? One problem with wood is that it will naturally degrade as water and insects work their way through it. Chalker-Scott suggests using naturally resistant types of wood, including cedar and juniper, which will not deteriorate as fast as other woods in contact with soil and soil-borne organisms.

Composite Lumber

Plastic plays an unfortunately large part in the maritime Northwest garden, and it pains me to recommend yet another use of it. I consider myself an environmentalist and conservationist, and I believe that we need to live lightly on the land, preserve our natural resources, and pass on the planet to the next generation in as good a form as possible.

My idealism is tempered by pragmatism when it comes to garden products, and that extends to lumber made with materials such as recycled plastic, which I think is a good second use of all the plastic generated in our culture. It is also a decent alternative to wood if you're building a raised bed in our climate, because it will not degrade when coming in contact with soil. It's a bit more expensive than wood but is cheaper than some of the other raised-bed products, and it has a long life and requires little maintenance. I've had two small composite-lumber raised beds in my yard for nearly a decade and have been satisfied with the performance of the product over time.

Composite lumber is primarily recycled plastic, although some manufacturers blend in other materials, such as sawdust or other wood waste. Trex, one of the earliest composite lumber companies, makes its planks from wood scrap, sawdust, and recycled plastic grocery bags. Orcaboard, made in Shoreline, Washington, just north of Seattle, uses high-density polyethylene (HDPE) plastic, the number-2 plastic used in milk jugs and other liquid containers. Commonly, these products include an ultraviolet (UV) stabilizer to prevent the material from breaking down in the sun, they come in different colors, and sometimes a wood grain is applied to the finish.

Raised beds made with composite lumber often come in kits, but you can also buy the materials separately. Many lumberyards and big-box building-supply stores carry some brand of it, and you can purchase plastic or metal corners to link the pieces. Longer boards often need lateral support stakes every few feet to prevent bowing; the products I've worked with are more flexible than wood.

Although composite lumber is flexible, it is also a very dense and hard material to cut or pierce. For a clean cut, use a sharp carbide blade on a circular saw and expect to sacrifice the blade to the project. Drill pilot holes and use sturdy, exterior-rated screws to fasten the pieces together.

I like to apply thin copper strips to my raised beds to organically repel slugs. The strips come with an adhesive backing that quickly fails, so I like to attach the copper to the raised bed with heavy staples. Trying to staple the material to my composite lumber has been challenging; even using a sturdy staple gun, the staples generally go in only halfway. Finish the job with a hammer.

Stackable Pavers, Bricks, Stone, or Urbanite

With more effort and a larger investment, you can build raised beds out of materials such as concrete blocks, stone, or bricks that have some significant advantages over any type of lumber. These hard materials add a grounding quality to the garden like nothing else. Plants grow and die and soil crumbles under the shovel's edge, but the hardscape is forever, aging and weathering at such an infinitely slow rate as to be unnoticeable. It is elemental, like sun, wind, and rain. It takes muscle to move it, and once it is settled, it stubbornly resists repositioning.

Stone can ratchet up the raised-bed effort and cost almost exponentially if you build decorative or architectural beds using stacked flagstone, building stone such as quartzite, river rock, or even poured concrete with a stone facade. Assuming that most of us food gardeners aren't creating raised beds for a spread in *Architectural Digest,* below are a few of the more accessible products.

Bricks are attractive and plentiful, especially if you or a neighbor is removing an old chimney. It can be labor-intensive and hazardous to chip away the mortar from old bricks, because the mortar might have contained asbestos. Look for a supply of clean bricks. Stacked two bricks high, they can suffice without mortar. They also are very attractive as edging, partially sunk into the shallow raised bed at an angle, pointed corners aiming for the sky.

I keep a supply of bricks stored around the yard that I lug from place to place when needed. They come in handy for keeping my wood cold frame off the soil or for weighing down the sheet plastic covering a bed. River rocks, from softball-size to bowling-ball size, serve a similar purpose.

Urbanite is a great material for the committed recycler's raised bed. Another name for it is

Urbanite, a.k.a. chunks of broken-up sidewalk, makes a rustic recycled wall.

rubble, but in this context, it's a bit more than that. A better description of it is well-chosen, manageable-sized, relatively consistent pieces of broken concrete. It might have been a sidewalk or a parking pad. Now, rather than haul it all to a concrete-recycling center where it is ground up and used again, simply reuse it, or have a big pile of it dropped off at your house. It's often pretty cheap and could even be free, if you know the person doing the yard remodeling. You might have to go and get it, though, which can present a significant barrier. That's a condition for many of these materials, and I offer a solution below.

Broken sidewalk chunks—excuse me, urbanite—can have a significant charm. It can have an exposed aggregate, a pebbly look, or wear patterns. It definitely arrives in unique shapes. When you stack it, you can try for a uniform, flat front to your wall, but even if you chisel off the odd protruding corners, you'll still have a wall with a lot of voids and unevenness. It takes more skill to stack, because it's difficult to get it in consistently flat and smooth tops and bottoms. It may require mortaring into place to make it sturdy and safe. We've used it for terraces in my yard and for a set of rustic steps cutting through the terraces, and we regularly get compliments from our generous friends.

Modular concrete wall blocks truly do multiple duty in my garden; I use them for my two main raised vegetable beds. These interlocking stackers are definitely a step up from cinder blocks. They're in the middle of the cost range and create a permanent bed with nice lines and a smooth top row that provides a lot of seating space for gardeners or visitors. And because they are uniform and create a nearly vertical wall, they provide more garden space than urbanite.

There are two tricks to using these: setting the base row, and hiring a neighbor kid to get them on site.

First, run a string line to mark the perimeter of your raised bed, driving stakes at each corner and closely spaced along an edge that will be curved, which can provide a pleasing result. Consult with the supplier as to how much of a curve can be used, or experiment with a few blocks. Excavate a trench along the string line into which you'll set the first course. For extra stability, plan on sinking the first blocks at least an inch below the height of the pathway around the bed. The excavated area should be hard-packed, and a layer of crushed base rock and/or sand helps level the blocks in place. The stone supply house will advise you on the right base material depending on the product chosen.

To get a plumb and level first course, use two spirit levels—a short one the depth of the wall and a longer one that spans at least three blocks along the length of the wall. Grade the base layer flat and level, then bring in the blocks. A borrowed pickup and a hired high-school kid (football players preferred) save time and your back. Set the first course slowly, checking often to see that it's going in flat and level and adjusting the base layer as needed. Once the first course is on, the wall will nearly build itself—well, with the help of the high-school lineman.

Rust-Inhibiting Metals

Galvanized troughs. All the rage with urban farmers in our region is the use of the galvanized trough for a raised bed. Formerly hauled out to the edge of a pasture to water the herd, galvanized troughs now provide slightly industrial architectural details to many Northwest urban gardens.

They have good benefits as raised beds. Their thin yet durable walls maximize planting space. They're usually 3–4 feet tall, a height that offers easy gardening to people who have problems bending over. Their shiny silver color can brighten up a drab winter landscape, although the metal does dull after a few seasons. And their curvy oval lines are pleasing. The only drawbacks to them are that some people don't like the down-home look and others say they're too small and you'd need a lot of them to get enough garden space—but for small yards with limited garden space, their size is a bonus.

Cor-Ten. A more sophisticated metal look comes from a weathering steel product called Cor-Ten. Manufactured by US Steel, it is a heavy, rolled sheet steel that has made its way from use on bridges and as structural steel to use in residential and commercial landscapes. It is much thicker and heavier than galvanized metal, but still provides a slim wall to hold in the soil. It can be formed with square corners or graceful curves, so landscape designers love it. What I like about it is that it weathers to a deep brown, and then the rusting virtually stops. It's expensive, but it would really make a statement in the garden.

Practicing season extension doesn't have to involve extreme efforts. Plopping down some hot caps is easy, although monitoring them while in use can be a commitment. Conversely, the challenge is all up-front when building a raised bed, but once it's finished, it will provide a warmer, easier-to-tend vegetable space. But there are more advanced techniques that will deliver greater rewards, allowing you to grow edibles year-round. Those more involved practices are covered in the next chapter.

COOL-SEASON KEYS TO TAKING EASY STEPS TO EXTEND THE GROWING SEASON

- Warm up and dry out soil by solarizing.
- Blanket plants with floating row cover.
- Protect single plants with cloches or hot caps.
- Build a raised bed for heat and better drainage.

8

Learning Advanced Practices for Season Extension

After just a few minutes in the garden on a maritime winter day, my fingers will be pretty well chilled to the bone. Insulated, rubber-coated gloves offer some relief as I get a bit of a gardening fix by pulling an odd weed, refilling the suet feeder, or cleaning up a forgotten pile of composted old stalks. I seek a trickle of vitamin D from the sun and fresh air as an antidote to Seasonal Affective Disorder, but relief from SADness on those cold,

The hoop house is an old technique, evidenced by this 18th-century wood frame with a paper covering. (Photo by Barbara Temple Lombardi, The Colonial Williamsburg Foundation)

short days can be fleeting. I perk right up, however, when it's time to harvest some dinner greens from under the cloche or lift the lid on the cold frame to see if the overwintering starts need water. Under the plastic hoop house or old glass window sash, I've created a different kind of winter, where our voluminous rain doesn't reach, our weak sun rays are concentrated, and my vegetable gardening continues, albeit on a small scale. Having my own food available nearly year-round right on the other side of my patio door makes the extra efforts of more advanced season-extension methods worthwhile.

More difficult season-extension techniques require building skills and close attention while using the devices you create. Protect tender winter vegetables and early spring sowings with larger cloches, and heat things up even more with cold frames. These popular garden structures also require hands-on involvement as the weather changes and plants grow. Ultimately, to get the most out of winter, build a hotbed under your cold frame or grow vegetables in a greenhouse.

From a bit of extra bed preparation in the spring to redesigning your garden and building a permanent greenhouse, advanced season extension offers many techniques to grow a little more food in a cool climate, keep the garden in production throughout the year, and harvest some food virtually year-round.

LARGER CLOCHES

Today, you can buy glass or plastic replicas of the French bell, but in the Northwest the more common cloching technique is to erect a "hoop house," a home-garden version of the dome-shaped "poly-tunnel" you see on many small farms.

The most common large cloche is built of wires or pipe bent into hoops and covered with clear polyethylene plastic. Former Washington State University Extension agent Holly Kennel calls them "covered wagons," and they do sort of make you think your garden gnomes are about to embark upon a trek down the Oregon Trail.

Positioning the Cloche

This type of cloche should be oriented so the long side is facing the sun, to allow maximum solar gain. Plan to put your hoop house alongside a hardscape pathway if possible for clean access, so you can check on the plants and growing conditions without getting very wet or dirty. It's best if the cloche is accessible from both sides, so you can remove and reinstall the cover as necessary.

The cloche works fine in an open garden bed, but even better on a wooden raised bed. You can set up the infrastructure once, and thereafter assembling the cloche is quick and easy.

To set up a hoop-house cloche, lay out the hoops along one long edge of the bed at your desired hoop spacing, so that the hoops are lined up nicely. Keep them parallel as you secure the other end of the hoop across the bed. This allows the clear sheet plastic cover to drape smoothly over the hoop assemblage.

If you're putting the cloche on a raised bed, make a mark every 18 or 24 inches with a permanent marker, or cut a shallow groove at those points if you have a wood bed, for a visual way to quickly set it up next time. If adding a cloche to a raised bed, you can even screw an eye hook or pound a U-shaped wire staple into each spot where the hoops will go. When you want to set up the cloche, slip the hoop ends through the hooks and down into the soil at least 6 inches to hold them in place.

Set boards or stone pavers along each end of the cloche so you can occasionally walk around the cloche without compacting the soil or getting muddy. It is, of course, ideal if you don't

A generous cloche of wood frame, wire mesh, and heavy plastic

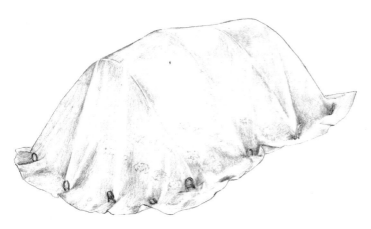

Garden staples can securely hold sheet plastic on a cloche.

have to step onto the garden soil at all, because any weight on the soil causes some compaction, which is detrimental to soil porosity and the health of the soil food web. If you must step on the bed, using a long board disperses your weight over a larger surface area.

Sizing Your Hoop House Cloche

Just as no two snowflakes are exactly alike, so too is each garden bed unique. You may have a small or odd-shaped space where you want to put a large cloche, while your friend with the community garden space has a nice, big rectangular bed. Maybe you just want a single row of lettuce, so you need a modest-sized cloche, but the community garden is growing a bushel of greens with intensive spacing, so they need a much bigger cloche. Here are some tips on calculating its size.

The cloche-covered bed should be no more than 4 feet across, for a couple of reasons. Any wider, and the plastic cover gets unwieldy and the cloche hoops too big. Wire or fiberglass hoops do not come in extremely long lengths, and even if you cut your own hoops from a roll, the gauge of

wire most commonly used is not stiff enough to create a high arc over a wider bed. Conversely, a low cloche with hoops close to the ground is good only for very small plants.

Almost as importantly, keep the bed narrow enough so that you can reach to the center when standing on either side. For many people, 3 feet is ideal and 4 feet is maximum.

The cloche needs to be large enough so you don't have to plant too close to the plastic cover, or the plants will squish up against the cloche and be deformed as they grow. Your effective gardening space for shorter plants starts 4–6 inches from the hoops. Rows that run parallel to the long side of the cloche are most efficient, with shorter vegetables along the edges and taller ones in the middle.

The hoop house should have a great enough arc that snow will easily slide off of it, another reason you don't want a cloche too close to the ground. A layer of overnight snow that collapses the cloche can crush the plants inside—and dash your winter gardening hopes with it.

Consider two factors when deciding on the height of the cloche: its width and the expected size of the plants (see the Sizing Your Hoop House sidebar). If you want to grow two rows of lettuce, for instance, your cloche can be 2 feet wide and does not need to be more than 10 inches high. Start each row 6 inches from the cloche sides, which will leave 6 inches between rows and 3 inches on each side when the lettuce is mature. Taller plants need more headroom and may also need to be farther from the hoops to allow them to spread out.

SIZING YOUR HOOP HOUSE

The hoop length and plastic sheet size of a large cloche are dependent upon the width of the bed and how high you want the center of your cloche to be.

BED WIDTH	PLANTING ROWS	HOOP LENGTH	CLOCHE CENTER HEIGHT	PLASTIC SHEET WIDTH
1 ft.	1	4 ft.	14 in.	4 ft.
1½ ft.	1 wide row	6 ft.	18 in.	5 ft.
2 ft.	2	4 ft.	10 in.	5 ft.
		5 ft.	14 in.	5 ft.
		5½ ft.	26 in.	6 ft.
		6 ft.	18 in.	6 ft.
		8 ft.	36 in.	8 ft.
3 ft.	2 wide rows	5 ft.	16 in.	5 ft.
		5½ ft.	22 in.	6 ft.
		6 ft.	18 in.	6 ft.
		8 ft.	33 in.	8 ft.
3½ ft.	3	5½ ft.	16 in.	6 ft.
		6 ft.	18 in.	8 ft.
		8 ft.	30 in.	8 ft.
4 ft.	3 wide rows	8 ft.	20 in.	10 ft.
		10 ft.	24 in.	12 ft.

Note: Measurements approximate for above-ground length; assume hoops have 6 inches in ground on each end

Setting the Hoops

Start with two or more long pieces of galvanized wire (about 0.110 inch thick, or nine gauge—a specialized product found at some hardware stores, mail-ordered, or purchased precut from cloche suppliers). Set them up in a series of half-circles, with each end of each half circle thrust into the ground.

To add stability, attach a straight rod or strip of wood between them, tied with twine to each hoop at the highest point, or one on each side two-thirds of the way up the arch. If adding these strengthening crosspieces, take care that they don't have any sharp ends or edges that would come into contact with the sheet plastic cover, because they would eventually (probably very quickly) poke holes in the stretched plastic.

PLASTIC SHEETING FOR LARGER CLOCHES

Cover your cloche hoops with plastic sheeting. Specialized products offer extra protection.

MATERIAL / SIZE	WIDTH	THICKNESS	LIGHT TRANSMIS-SION	COST PER LENGTH	SUPPLIER	NOTES
Greenhouse Poly Cover	15½ ft.	6 mil	90%	25 ft. $79; 50 ft. $149; 75 ft. $225	Charley's Greenhouse	Has UV protection, infrared component
Woven Poly Cover	12 ft.	8 mil	85%	$4.50/linear ft.	Charley's Greenhouse	Used to protect from extreme weather, but also good for plants
Dura Film Super 4	16 ft.	6 mil	91.5%	50 ft. $170	Online suppliers	Has UV, infrared; Made by AT Films
Warp's Carry Home Coverall	10 ft.; 15 ft.; 20 ft.	4 mil	*	10 ft. x 25 ft. $16; 15 ft. x 25 ft. $24; 20 ft. x 25 ft. $32	Home-improvement centers	Standard, construction-grade; no UV, infrared
SunMaster Greenhouse Film	10 ft.	6 mil	92%	$1.30/ linear ft. plus cut charge	Online retailers	Has UV, infrared; made by Lumite
Tufflite Green-house Poly	20 ft.	6 mil	91%	$3.49/linear ft. (in 5 ft. increments)		
Peaceful Valley Farm & Garden						Has UV, infrared; made by Berry Plastics

*Details not available

Note: Suppliers and prices accurate as of spring 2012

Buying the Right Plastic

You can purchase basic four- or six-mil clear polyethylene plastic sheeting in rolls at a big-box hardware store, and that will work OK for a larger cloche covering. But there is a specially made greenhouse plastic that works better. Although it's initially more expensive, plastic for this specific purpose has benefits. It is manufactured with an extra layer of film within the plastic to allow the passage of infrared light but to block its release, thus keeping the inside of the cloche warmer after a day of sun. Also, greenhouse plastics are "UV protected," which means they have another layer that slows breakdown of the film from ultraviolet light, a prime cause of plastic degradation. Greenhouse plastic sheeting with UV protection should last multiple seasons, while basic uncoated plastic may last only one or two years before it begins to break down because of the effects of the sun.

Different manufacturers have proprietary methods of creating greenhouse plastics, but thickness and light transmission are comparable.

Sizing and Securing the Plastic

Once the hoops are in place, cut a piece of the plastic sheeting to drape over the hoops. It should be large enough on the sides and ends to reach the ground and leave at least 1 foot flat on the ground. That will give you enough material to work with to hold down the edges. Covering the cloche is a job best done with two people on a calm day. If a friend isn't handy, use a board or rocks to hold down one side of the plastic while you drape it and measure.

Once the plastic is positioned and sized, pull it off, lay it out flat to cut it, then position it squarely over the hoops again before anchoring it.

Attaching the plastic sheeting to the hoops and holding it down can be done in a number of ways:

Wire hoops and vented plastic provide a light cover as the garden warms in spring.

- Soil covering the plastic overhang, which is laid in a trench
- Bricks or boards laid on the plastic
- Ground staples hammered through the plastic
- Single strips of board with the plastic stapled to it
- Double strips of board with the plastic sandwiched between it
- Office-supply-store binder clips or clothespins clamping the plastic to the hoops

Burying the edges of the plastic. This option is not ideal for a bed that will be tended regularly, because the plastic has to be pulled up on at least two sides whenever you want to open the cloche. Digging into the soil every time you want to rebury the cloche edges is a muddy, messy project.

Using ground staples. For many years, I held down my cloche plastic with bricks and boards, but more recently, I have taken to ground staples as handy, lightweight alternatives. The ground staple is a large, U-shaped wire, usually heavy enough steel that it is pretty stiff and not easily bent. It is

positioned over the plastic and poked through it, then driven into the ground. Use either the heel of your hand or, if the ground is resistant, a rubber mallet. I have a set of ground staples with an extra circular ring at the top, which makes them easier to remove.

The staple should be inserted until the bottom edge of the U is flat on the ground, securely holding down the plastic. Position them every 12–18 inches, depending on the spacing of your hoops, the windiness of your site, and whether you also use stones or boards to hold down the plastic. I position one at the base of each hoop.

I find that in most of my garden beds, the soil is loose enough that I don't need to use a mallet, and the staples go in by hand. But having a good, loose tilth to your soil is also a drawback for using staples, because they can work their way out of the soil more easily in windy conditions, and they might not hold the plastic as securely.

The other drawback to staples is that you must poke holes in your plastic sheeting. As a result, you will want to reinsert the staples into the same holes as much as possible. Even so, you end up having a series of holes along the edges of the plastic cover. Also, in a windy situation, the plastic holes can eventually be enlarged or torn by the repeated pulling effects of wind gusts.

Even with all these potential small problems, ground staples are an efficient and handy way to keep the plastic held over your cloche.

Attaching wood strips. Attaching wood to the edges of the plastic sheeting gives a clean look, and the wood strips help hold the plastic in place when you raise one side of the cloche. (This method is shown in the Hoop-House Cloche building project in the Appendix.)

Although it is a bit more work to assemble, I like the look of a wood-trimmed cloche. The main drawback to using wood strips on the edges is that when you take the cloche down, the wood attached to the plastic makes the plastic sheeting a bit more unwieldy to store. Also, it is not as tight a fit as you can get with clips or hold-downs such as bricks.

If you want an extra-tight fit over the hoops, or if your garden is subject to high winds, you might still need a couple of bricks on top of the wood slats to keep the wind from getting up under the cloche and blowing up its sides.

Using clips. Another way to hold the plastic sheeting on the hoops is probably the simplest and the most portable. Simply drape the plastic over the hoops, weight it down around the edges, and secure it to the hoops with binder clips, also known as alligator clips. These clips made of black metal and stainless steel are used to hold sheaves of paper together. They come in many sizes at office-supply stores. One drawback: the metal eventually becomes rusty and hard to use, leaving a rusty stain on the edge of the plastic sheeting. Wooden clothespins are an acceptable alternative, but they do not clamp down as securely.

When I use binder clips, I install two or three clips on each hoop, but I also weight down the edges

---

An Environmental Note: Ditching PVC Hoops

For decades, the standard homemade cloche design has included lengths of white PVC pipe, the material used by plumbers. Recently there has been a welcome shift in cloche design made possible by more commonly available alternatives to PVC. It has caused me to breathe a sigh of relief.

I've never liked the look of the white plastic tubes arcing over my garden bed, and I've grown more and more aware of the serious environmental problems with PVC. Toxic chemicals are used in its manufacture and released in its disposal, one of the most voluminous categories being dioxins, which are known to be carcinogenic and disrupt hormones, and another being phthalates, which disrupt the endocrine system. As my awareness has been raised, I've come to resent those white hoops even more and not want them anywhere near my organic vegetables, even though the PVC pipe would itself seem unlikely to break down and leach into my food.

Many commercial cloche kits are built with PVC; you can also certainly view my cloche plans and substitute PVC for the materials I suggest. However, winter gardening uses enough other plastics (as we all do in our daily lives), so I want to draw the line and say goodbye to the PVC hoops.

For extensive resources on the problems with PVC, see the nonprofit Center for Health, Environment, and Justice (www.chej.org).

of the plastic with bricks or boards, because I have found that strong winds can pick up the edge of the plastic (which then flaps or tears) and wreak havoc on the atmosphere inside the cloche. Because I want to keep my plants warm and dry under the cloche, I secure all the edges to the ground. This arrangement is not the most convenient; when pulling off the sheeting, it takes a bit more time and effort to remove all the rocks and clips.

Other Hoop Materials

The basic hoop house is just a chicken scratch on the surface of a yard full of creative cloche designs. And galvanized wire is far from the only choice for hoops. Here are some alternative materials, with their relative benefits:

Fiberglass hoops. Thin and flexible, these straight rods are similar to wire hoops except they retain their shape a bit better when flexed into a hoop. Wire will deform with repeated use, which affects aesthetics more than function, but the fiberglass springs back into its straight form when pulled from the bed.

Unfortunately, I have found fiberglass hoops only in relatively short 60-inch lengths, which are useful only for narrow beds or cloches with a somewhat low center height. If bent into too tight a hoop, they will break. I've also found them available only through mail-order garden-supply companies, although I hope nurseries will begin to carry them.

Bamboo hoops. Long bamboo culms cut and bent into hoop shapes make an attractive cloche. Look for 10- to 15-foot pieces, at least 1/2 inch in diameter. After cutting them to length, trim off all leaves and as much of the leaf-node brackets as possible. Also trim the top 1–2 feet off the culm, because that is too thin to use. Tie a small bundle of culms together with twine on each end and

Zip ties can hold cloche wire to polyethylene hoops.

multiple spots along the length, then bend them into a half circle. Prop them securely into a spot where they can sit and dry for a few months before use. When they are dry enough to hold their shape, untie them and sand off any sharp edges where the leaf nodes were, so the plastic won't rip when stretched over the hoops.

Black polyethylene tubing. The flexible tubing used as the main line in aboveground drip irrigation systems can work for cloches, although it tends to collapse with too much weight. It also softens when exposed to UV, so it could collapse after being warmed by the sun. With proper support, though, it can be a fine alternative. Space the hoops 12–18 inches apart, as you would galvanized wire, and connect them with a center support.

Also, attach the hoops to rebar posts driven half-way into the soil and extending out of the ground. You can get 1/2-inch rebar rods cut into 2- or 4-foot lengths at the big-box hardware stores. Get the longer rods for more stability if you have loose, sandy soil.

Welded wire mesh. This product, which comes in rolls laid out in a grid pattern, is used as fencing, but it can provide a consistent hoop shape with good support for the plastic cover. The mesh is generally heavier than chicken wire, but the gauge of the metal is thinner than the galvanized wire hoop material. It comes painted, galvanized, or unfinished, but the third option rusts, so is not recommended.

The drawback to wire mesh is that there may be sharp edges at the weld points, which will rip holes in the plastic cover stretched over it. If the product is smooth with no sharp edges, it will work well. Here are some other tips for wire mesh:

- Connect wire mesh to black polyethylene tubing with zip ties to create a sturdy assemblage. (See the Appendix for a building plan.)
- Keep this frame on the bed all year for different uses. In summer you can drape shade cloth over it or use it as a trellis for growing cucumbers or squash.

Raised beds in winter on a restaurant rooftop garden in Portland

Wood. Create a cloche with wood lath or a 1-by-2-inch frame, or incorporate wood into parts of your design:

- Build a wood frame for the sides of the cloche, and attach wire hoops or wire mesh to the top to create the inverted U shape.
- Build an entire wood frame with a peaked roof instead of a hoop shape. This design is close to being a cold frame, but if plastic sheeting is stapled to the frame, it functions more like a cloche, because it won't warm the soil as much as if it had the cold frame's glass top.
- If you are a woodworker, you might be able to bend wood strips into hoop shapes. That is done with thin wood soaked in water to soften it, then clamped into a shape and left to dry. I know a gardener who uses slats from wine barrels as hoops—very attractive and durable.

Other metal hoops. Commercial cloche kits use galvanized tubular metal material, but you could fabricate these yourself if you have a specialized tubing bender. Or you could use copper water

Commercial cloches often come with internal wire frames and zippered openings.

tubing or metal electrical conduit, which also would require a pipe-bending or conduit-bending tool. These options also might be more expensive than the other materials, especially the copper. A copper frame also could be constructed with rigid copper pipe, using elbows and corners, and it certainly would be more attractive than some of the other options. However, you would want your copper cloche to be in a location protected from theft, as copper has a significant scrap salvage value these days.

COLD FRAME: THE ULTIMATE REMOVABLE COVER

A few pieces of wood, some plastic, an old window, and a bit of cleverness in connecting them— those simple elements can be combined to create a most useful cool-season gardening tool: the cold frame. It is a great season-extending device to start heat-loving crops in the spring soil, is useful for cultivating seedlings as they grow in flats or pots, and can be used again in the cold season to overwinter vegetables or half-hardy potted plants.

Just as with the cloche, the cold frame offers different uses during different times of the year. In early winter and into the new year, use your cold frame to protect tender potted plants. It keeps them out of the howling wind and relentless rain, in an environment that's at least a few degrees warmer than the frigid outdoors. You can also boost a tender plant's chances of surviving by digging a hole in the bed under the cold frame and sinking the plant, pot and all, into the hole, then filling in around the pot with soil, adding a top layer of leaves or straw to further nestle it in for a winter sleep—a process *Rodale's* calls "hilling in."

In January and February, move your tender plants out, perhaps into a cloche if they still need

A rigid polycarbonate cold frame at Oregon Tilth

protection, and use the cold frame to grow seedlings you have started indoors. That gives you a head start on the spring season. In fact, the cold frame can turn late winter into early spring.

For instance, lettuce and other cool-season greens need a temperature of just 40–45°F to sprout. But during the short, coldest days of winter in the maritime Northwest, when the daytime air temperature outside barely reaches 40, it's unlikely your soil will hit that mark. Our weak daylight won't raise soil temperatures much either. Even under a cold frame, it might be tough to start seedlings off on a robust life. But if your cold frame

A classic cold frame with wood sides and repurposed window sashes, in a flower show display

is set up and ready to go, you can put it to work soon after your seedlings sprout.

Consider this three- or four-stage process to use a cold frame to start your growing year:

Stage 1: Start seeds of cool-tolerant vegetables in flats with a heat mat and grow lights as outlined in chapter 5, and get the seedlings growing robustly. Once they have a couple sets of true leaves, begin the process of hardening them to the outdoor environment. They have to be only "half-hardened," actually, because they'll go from your warm house to your somewhat-warm cold frame. Set them out during the day for a few days in the cold frame, which is warmed by the sun, but bring them indoors again at night. After three or four days, unless the weather has taken a sharp turn toward arctic, you can then leave them out in the frame overnight.

Stage 2: Continue to grow these starts in their pots in the cold frame. The lengthening days will provide more light, and your frame will offer more warmth. Monitor the seedlings closely for water needs. Soil should remain moist but not soggy. Also make sure to vent the frame on any unusually warm or sunny days, so you don't accidentally cook your tiny plants. If the starts continue to grow in the cold frame, they will outgrow their small seed-flat cells. On a nice day, pot them up into 4-inch pots.

Stage 3: If the outdoor temperatures are rising reliably and the nights are not dropping below about 40°F, consider planting the starts out into the garden. Or you can move them into a cloche, which can

eventually be removed if you want. That gives you more space in your cold frame for the next batch of seedlings.

Stage 4: Because your cold frame has been drying out the soil under it, you could move your seedlings directly from their flats into the soil under the cold frame. Closely monitor conditions inside the frame daily for heat and water, venting it and watering the seedlings as necessary. The benefit is that the cold-frame soil won't dry out as fast as the soil in small pots in the frame.

The Basic Cold Frame

A cold frame generally has a rigid structure compared to the cloche's flexible one. A cold frame is often built of wood with a top made of glass or rigid clear plastic. There are many variations on this theme, and below I offer three common designs and describe some possible departures from those designs. In this section, I offer general pointers on building different designs, and in the Appendix is a full-blown building project of a wooden raised bed and cold frame.

A cold frame can be used to shelter tender potted plants or new starts.

Before starting to build, though, visualize the finished product: a tilted pane of glass or plastic sits upon a sturdy base. The top is removable or easy to lift for access into the box. You also must be able to prop the top open for venting. The angle is set to get maximum sun inside the box. Ideally, the lower front side of the cold frame faces south, and the higher back side faces toward the north. Additional considerations include the following:

A large—and stylish—cold frame at the Fort Mason Community Garden in San Francisco

- Perhaps paint the wood of the cold frame for weather resistance. Use a light color for more reflectivity onto the plants. That can also provide some eye-catching color in your garden.
- If you use lightweight wood and plastic for the top, use bricks or a board to hold it down to protect against the wind.
- For more insulation during your coldest winter days, cut pieces of rigid foam insulation, the type with a silver reflective material on one side, to the size of each wall and place it on the inside of the box, with the reflective side facing in.
- You can also toss a blanket over the whole thing on a cold night and remove it during the day.
- Another nice addition to the structure is a handle screwed onto the front of each window frame.
- If the cold frame will be used directly on the garden bed, lay a brick or stone base on which to set it; ground contact with the frame will cause much faster rot, with the wood frame lasting perhaps only two seasons rather than eight to ten.
- I always take my cold frames apart and store them under cover when not in use, which greatly extends their life. Also, if they're properly assembled, you should be able to replace rotting wood or other parts as needed without much further effort.

I also offer this caveat: You do not need to be a carpenter to build a cold frame. Nor do you have to remodel your house so you can take the old windows out to the garden. There are simple ways to "build" this device without ever picking up a screw gun or a hammer, and the main element of a cold frame—the old window—can easily be found through companies that reclaim building parts.

Start with a Salvaged Window Sash

To begin creating your cold frame, you'll probably want a salvaged window sash for the top. An old glass window in its frame is the ideal beginning. Salvaged windows are plentiful, because Americans do so much home remodeling. Also for that reason, old windows are often cheap or free—my local store charges four dollars per pane for the windows, and even has a bargain rack with cheaper ones! And when you reuse an old window, you are

Go window shopping at a recycled building materials store.

discovery! There are many types, brands, and grades of plastic, so it might take some investigation to know what you want and a piece of luck if you're hoping to find used pieces that are in good shape. Plastic fades, scratches, or gets cloudy, so look for something that is as see-through as possible.

When sourcing out the materials for the top, keep an open mind and, as you hold up a likely candidate at a yard sale, thrift store, or junkyard, try to picture how you'd use it in the garden. The cold-frame top simply needs to be something that will let a lot of light through to the plants below.

doing your municipal landfill a favor by keeping it out of the waste stream, at least for a while.

Glass offers the most transparency and longevity (although it is fragile), so I consider it the best choice. Usually, old windows are made of single-pane glass, as opposed to today's high-tech versions with multiple panes and insulating gases injected between them.

Plastic is lighter weight and more durable than glass, and it's less likely to crack or shatter. You can find rigid plastic panels of fiberglass, polycarbonate, or acrylic, like the material used in old skylights. In fact, an old skylight is a wonderful

A salvaged skylight covers a raised bed

One criterion might be that it has as much clear area as possible and a thin frame, because a heavy, thick frame will block some of the available light and make the piece more unwieldy.

To find the perfect top, haunt the recycled building-materials stores, those places where salvaged materials are stacked up and just waiting for a new life. These "second-use" stores always have a wonderful variety of windows, but most of these windows are unusable for cold frames. Many are too fancy and, thus, too costly to justify setting out in the yard. Odd sizes are hard to work with; very old windows were made with solid wood that is often too heavy. Some have "divided lights"— many panes of glass in a large frame, separated by wood mullions. These can be difficult to use as a cold frame because the interior wood frames can shadow the bed and reduce the amount of sun exposure to the ground below. The mullions can also be hard to keep painted, and there are many more puttied edges to keep in good condition.

You might find glass doors from old kitchen cabinets, which generally are made of thinner, lighter material than external windows, although they tend to be smaller. You also might find patio doors or old storm doors that would work, although they might be too large.

Paw through the racks of old windows and doors, looking for something that is light enough for you to lift and carry easily, as well as approximately the right size for your available garden bed. Measure the bed first, then visit the store with tape measure in hand. It's like the search done by Goldilocks in the nursery rhyme when she tried to find the best bed: you need the one that is "just right."

A word about environmental issues: Old windows can contain hazardous substances. The old glazer's putty commonly contained asbestos, which is a problem if you sand it and particles become airborne. Window frames might also be covered in lead paint, which is a significant issue if you use the old frame in your garden. Lead was outlawed as a paint additive in the United States in 1978, but before then it was commonly used. The heavy metal is toxic to humans and pets. According to the health experts at the Mayo Clinic (www.mayoclinic.com), even a small amount can result in lead poisoning, which causes serious health effects and, at high levels, can be fatal. "Children under the age of six are especially vulnerable to lead poisoning, which can severely affect mental and physical development," advises the clinic on its website, adding that lead-based paint in old buildings and lead-contaminated soils are primary ways children come in contact with lead.

The best lead-avoidance technique is to find unpainted windows in metal or wood frames. The wood ones might have a wood stain and varnish on them, but these should be lead-free. If the frame is painted, research how to encapsulate or remove that paint safely. Then repaint the bare wood with a modern, lead-free paint. Encapsulate the old glazing with paint as well. If it must be removed, consult your local environmental agency for instructions on how to do it safely.

Using metal-framed windows avoids those problems and could be the best choice for other reasons, too. Metal windows have great advantages in the garden. They generally won't rust and can be spray-painted to jazz them up a bit. A metal frame is typically lighter weight than a wood one and thinner, so it meets both of a gardener's primary requirements: easy to lift and move, and lets the most possible light through. Sometimes you can find a double-pane metal window in a sliding frame that makes venting the cold frame a literal breeze.

Venting and easy access are both challenges that should be considered when window-shopping. Cool-season gardeners need to open their cold frame regularly to pull weeds, check the soil temperature and moisture levels, plant, water, and harvest. You also need to vent the cold frame on warm days to prevent your plants from wilting or being cooked in an overheated box. With a single wood-frame window, that means installing an automatic vent control, propping up the top, or lifting the top completely off the frame. But with a metal sliding window, you can leave it in place and slide it open a bit to vent or a lot to tend the bed. Yes, you have to open and close it manually, and the automatic opener has its appeal. There is one other drawback to metal windows: you may have

a hard time finding them. One salvage expert told me that she rarely purchases them, or even comes across them, because they often don't survive removal from a building, as they end up bent and unusable. Still, the hunt and discovery are half the fun of building with recycled products.

It takes methodical digging to reveal the best candidates. The ideal windows should have these features:

- sturdy frames with clear, unbroken glass and not very much hardware such as hinges or fancy handles.
- solid lines of putty holding the glass in place, not cracking or separating from the frame or the glass.

Shop Recycled

We waste an amazing amount of stuff. I don't mean you and me, necessarily, but we, as a society. The topic has launched a hundred documentaries, as well as a huge industry that is now known as "waste management." It's an appropriate term, because so much of what we throw away is beyond the definition of garbage.

But, just as much as some people like to shop and replace their perfectly good things with the latest and costliest, others thrill to the hunt of something old that can be remade into something useful. My brain agitates crazily like an old washing machine when I walk through the secondhand stores. Sometimes I take home a box of treasures; other times I leave with just ideas.

Recently I went hunting at the RE Store in Seattle, situated in the Ballard neighborhood under a richly drawn two-story mural that covers its facade. Bins of glass doorknobs

beckoned just inside the door. Those would make colorful tops to a bamboo windbreak along the edge of the garden. Clear globes that once hung over ceiling lights could—the larger ones, anyway— be repurposed into small cloche bells to put over seedlings. If they have a center hole to screw on the fixture, all the better; fill it with a wine cork, which can be removed for a vent on a warm day. Stainless-steel wire shelves that once held kitchen spices could be screwed to a fence wall to hold pots of herbs, fresh and handy for snipping. But that is just the front room. Consider these areas:

The window department: This is surely the source of the most useful cool-season gardening materials, because a couple of old window sashes gets you two-thirds of the way to a new cold frame. See the section on cold frames for suggestions on how to choose old windows.

The metal bin: People toss out old deck-railing systems, which often are made of tubular steel

- smooth frame surfaces, either unpainted (best) or paint that is not peeling (see earlier discussion on lead paint); extremely weathered, rough wood or scratched-up metal can be very uncomfortable to handle and can degrade much faster in the garden.
- a width that fits over a cold-frame base the dimensions of your bed (say, 4 feet wide maximum) or at angles if tilted together (2½ or 3 feet).
- a length that meets the needs of your bed but can still be moved easily (say, 3–5 feet for a long, narrow bed).
- light enough to lift, carry, and store easily (they probably won't be in your garden the entire year).

If you're building a large cold frame, loo[...] of windows that match. You might wan[...] them side by side on a long bed. For yea[...] used a pair of wood frames that came f[...] own home's remodel. I was going to ma[...] cold frame, but when the glass broke i[...] them, I removed it and laid one on top[...] adding hinges to the back. The result [...] movable lid. I then built the cold-fram[...] to the dimensions of the window, out[...] inch wood.

For a lean-to-style cold frame, I fo[...] matching windows that were rather l[...] row. I bought some hollow galvanize[...] lengths that I could drive into the gr[...] and prop the windows against. Setti[...]

and in perfectly good shape. They make great trellises or, propped up on their sides, can even be the base for a cold frame. Lean one against a wall, prop windows on it, and you have a sturdy cold frame.

Structural framing: Solid old lumber is abundant, and it is so dense and dry that it would last a long time as a raised bed. But it may also be so hard that it will dull a saw blade and must be predrilled to be fastened together.

The yard: Old posts from fencing and tents are often discarded, and if you have access to a metal-bending tool, you can use these to make a hoop-house cloche. Or buy the long straight pieces, cut them up, and purchase the connectors and angles to build a minigreenhouse. If you're lucky, you might find a bin of connectors as well!

Furniture: On a garden tour in a recent summer, I saw a miniature raised bed made of an old bedroom dresser drawer, painted s[...] and it looked perfectly in place sitt[...] rusty metal table. It eventually will [...] but meanwhile it makes a stellar s[...] Imagine a series of drawers, artfull[...] or stacked at angles, all filled with [...] handles facing out, and squash vin[...] down their sides.

Cabinetry: Metal drawers mig[...] better. At one recycled-materials [...] a stack of gray metal cubes, 2 fee[...] that would be perfect lining a wa[...] see old gym lockers, and I've see[...] in a garden as a tool shed, but I [...] it would look as a raised bed, lai[...] with the door permanently prop[...] removed. Especially good woul[...] bins, perhaps from some factor[...] hardware store. Drill a few drai[...] start growing!

pes per side, set at angles to meet at the height
the windows, resulted in an A-frame cold frame
g enough for one long row. I cut two triangles
sturdy, six-mil plastic to cover the ends, which
eps the heat in and protects from wind.

Once you have your old window for the top, it's
ne to start building the cold frame. The easiest
y to do it is to plop the old window on top of
terials that you have around the garden. A stur-
r but lightweight option is a plastic-wrapped
that fits over a wooden raised bed. More
olved is a freestanding box with vents and a
ged lid. Each one of these designs, along with
resting variations, are detailed below.

ld a Cold Frame Without Tools

you dangerous with a screw gun or all thumbs
a hammer? If your image of a construction
ect includes bleeding fingers and a trip to the
rgency room, don't give up on the idea of a cold
e. You can make one without joining wood
eaking up a relationship. A cold frame is an
. recycling project. Think like a kid and start
acking a few things that have been sitting
nd the yard:

y bales are great insulators, as are burlap or
stic bags filled with gathered leaves.
s of mulch can serve double duty before
ng opened and spread on the garden.
a stack of firewood or larger stems from a
-pruning job.
her up stray bricks, concrete blocks, boards,
roken-concrete pavers.
cate large black plastic pots that had been
ving annuals; remove the plants but leave
n filled with soil.
organized with the very prim-and-proper
kable pavers sold at the big-box home stores.

Any of those materials can be formed into a cold
frame base in just a few minutes. The trick is to
have a vision and the available space. Here's how:

1. Start with your hay bale or a stack of three large
   bags of compost as the back wall. You might
   want to drive some supporting stakes into the
   ground on both sides of the stacked compost
   bags to make them more stable.

2. For the front, gather some concrete blocks.
   The hollow ones are lighter and easier to move;
   broken-concrete pavers made from a former
   sidewalk are great recycled materials but can be
   uneven heights, and usually the bottom side is
   not smooth, so they are more challenging to get
   level and stable. Place these as your front wall,
   spaced so that the window top will sit securely
   on both the front and the back. Bear in mind that
   you want the top to slant downward from back to
   front so the front wall should be one-quarter to
   one-half the height of the back. The angled top,
   besides allowing in more light, will let rain run
   off easily, so the moisture won't rust the metal
   frame or rot the wood frame of the window top.

3. Once your front and back walls are built, put
   the top in place and stand back. Evaluate the
   angle and make sure the top is secure. Look
   down at the bed through the top to make sure
   it's centered on the soil you want to use. These
   materials take up a lot of space in the garden, so
   you might want to adjust them to get the most
   use out of the bed space.

4. When you're satisfied with the shape, location,
   and stability, then construct the sides. Again,
   you could simply stack up bags of compost,
   bricks, or concrete pavers. Line up a row of
   black plastic pots wrapped in plastic sheeting
   that is tied on with twine. Find boards that
   would cover the space tipped on their sides, and

A simple cold frame: leaning windows surrounded by straw

drive stakes into the ground to keep them in place. The goal is to securely block the openings on each side to keep the weather out. That also keeps the warmer microclimate inside the cold frame. Pay particular attention to the corners where the materials meet, and try to plug up any holes. Burlap bags filled with compost, leaves, or even weeds are great for that use, because they can be molded into shapes that fit the angled side wall openings.

The beauty of the found-object cold frame might be a bit elusive. A cobbled-together mix of materials can look messy and more like a junk pile than a winter garden. A bit of extra effort to make it tidy can result in a funky, arty look. Winter gardeners can see past the mess of materials and find the beauty in the practicality of their homemade plant protector, but your neighbors may not get it. The form will matter less than the function when you harvest winter lettuces or sprout those peas extra early.

Make a Self-Supporting A-Frame

Another nonbuilt design is the A-frame, made with two or more windows. It helps if they are about the same size and if they're rectangular rather than square. You'll also need some stakes to drive into the ground at angles across the bed you plan to cover. These could be 1-by-2-inch or 2-by-2-inch wood, sturdy bamboo, rebar, or other metal rods. You'll need two per window. Picture the long sides of a capital A that you'll be creating when you drive the stakes into the ground.

1. Measure the length of the window, then position the stakes to be 4 inches in from each end of the window length.
2. Drive the stakes into the soil, deeply if your window is large or heavy, or at least 6 inches to support a lightweight window.
3. The tops of the stakes should meet, as do the long strokes of the letter A, so that one stake props against the other. The tops also can continue beyond where they cross each other, as long as they are lashed together for support.
4. Center the windows up against the stakes; they will hang over a couple of inches on each end. For very long windows or a door, use more stakes to fill in along each side for better support. For longer pieces, you might want supports every 24–30 inches. When you lay the window up against the stakes, you'll know very quickly whether the stakes are sturdy and secure enough to support it.

The A-frame design is often built without fastening together any of the parts, with the weight of the windows holding themselves in place. In a windy area, though, you can drive stakes into the ground outside the window, too, at the same angle.

This type of cold frame also has open ends, which is not the best choice for maximum cold-frame effect. To make this into a true greenhouse, you'll need to close the ends. That can be done by placing a board against each end that's large

Single-row triangle cloches

enough to cover it, then driving a stake along the outside edge of the board to hold it in place. You could cut a board or rigid plastic to the right triangular size to fill that space. Or even take heavy sheet plastic and staple it onto one window frame, then pull it across the opening and stake it down on the other side. By not stapling both sides, you will be able to open it easily to gain access to the cold frame or to lift the windows away.

On a recent visit to a Lake Oswego, Oregon, community garden, I was delighted to see a creative departure on this A-frame style (see photo above). When I asked the garden leaders about the design, they said it had been done by a local Boy Scout working on an Eagle Scout project. His design works great for a single row crop. The design is basically a rectangular box that sits flat on the ground, with angled pieces of wood at each end that meet to form a triangle, and the whole thing is covered in corrugated plastic sheeting. See the Appendix for a building project that is my take on this design.

The Boy Scout's creation was the result of adding a bit of carpentry skill to the A-frame design concept. If you're a little bit handy with wood and basic tools, you too can construct a cold frame that will serve your garden's needs. If you're a woodworking expert, by all means create garden structures that are beautifully formed, with symmetrical lines and tight-fitting joinery. But if you're not—don't stress about it! My garden has taught me that nature itself often settles for "make do" over perfection, and sometimes the strangest-looking, oddly growing plants produce the most delectable results. So, too, should your construction efforts be focused on the functionality (and even the funkiness) over the form. Your plants won't notice the imperfections. Your visitors might think they add character. And good enough will do.

Build a Cold Frame Atop a Raised Bed

Chapter 7 suggests making a raised bed from wood, which gives you the opportunity to attach a cold frame or a cloche to it. With a cloche, it's a matter of attaching connecting hardware to the vertical inside wall of the raised bed so that you can slip the cloche hoops through to anchor them. But attaching a cold frame onto a wooden raised bed takes a little more planning. You can make the cold frame fit inside the frame of the bed or sit on top of it. It can be freestanding or temporarily or permanently attached. The final design will be dictated by the gardener's needs, by the size and materials of the raised bed, and whether you want

A productive tall raised bed topped by a cold frame

The raised bed that holds this cold frame is tall, about 30 inches, and the wooden cold-frame structure is permanently attached to it. The walls of the cold frame bring the height of the box up another 10 inches in front and nearly 20 in back (because, of course, the back must be higher than the front to create the sloping top that captures more solar rays and allows rain to run off). The soil level is at the raised bed height, so with the cold frame on top, it's a long reach into the bed to plant, weed, or harvest. I guess that doesn't pose a problem for the tall owner, but it's a lesson: make sure whatever you build will fit your stature. You want to be able to easily reach the soil level at the back of the bed.

The cleverest part of the community gardener's tall cold frame is what he did for the lid. You can use many types of transparent materials for the lid: old windows, sheets of rigid polycarbonate, stiff acrylic plastic, even heavy plastic sheeting, stretched tautly over a wood frame. This gardener used heavy acrylic sheeting, sturdy but with enough flexibility to bend a bit. It fits nicely into wood grooves on the front and back walls of the lid. With a handle screwed to the center of each piece, he can easily snap these pieces into place, take them off, or even slide them to the side to reach the bed. When he wants the bed to go lid-less in summer, the lightweight panels are easily removed for storage.

In a similar vein, I have seen old glass window sashes and skylights set on top of a raised bed built to their dimensions. Often the top is attached to the back wall of the raised bed with hinges. A stick is most commonly used to prop open the tops for venting on a warm day, but some of the nicer designs have wood supports attached both to the box and the lid to keep the lid from being flung open by gusting winds.

the cold frame to sit on the bed year-round.

To build efficiently, you'll need a couple of small power tools—a circular saw and a screw gun with driver bits and drill bits. Along with a tape measure, you'll need a straightedge, a T square, and a sliding T bevel to chart a few angle cuts. The raised bed and cold frame mostly are put together with screws, because eventually you will need to replace boards that rot from being in contact with moisture and soil.

Perhaps the most effective one I've seen was built by a gardener at the Picardo P-Patch in Seattle (see photo above). It's spacious and sturdy.

One of the most important building steps is to get the lid set at the proper angle. The back of the lid should be at least 6 inches higher than the front wall to create at least a ten-degree angle, which sheds rain and gains more light. The angle can be greater, up to forty-five degrees.

In the Appendix, I offer instructions on building a complete raised bed–cold frame combination. If constructing a cold frame seems like a big undertaking, consider the effort versus the results. When you are finished, you will have a durable device that greatly expands your growing capability in the coldest season and should last for many years.

RADIATE VEGGIE GROWTH WITH A HOTBED

There's a technique to get even more out of your cold frame, useful for those who want to maximize production year-round or keep very tender, heat-loving plants alive throughout the winter. It's called a hotbed, and it is a centuries-old method, but of course it has been given a makeover by modern technology.

I had read about hotbeds in old gardening books, dating to the 1700s, but I had never tried it or talked with any gardeners who had, until I met Wesley Greene. He's a garden historian, a job that allows him to be that bridge between old and new. The aptly named Greene is in charge of the food gardens at Colonial Williamsburg in Virginia.

Colonial Williamsburg, according to its mission statement, was Great Britain's "largest, wealthiest, and most populous outpost of empire in the New World," and today a nonprofit foundation operates the historic 301-acre town site as "the world's largest living history museum." The restored town takes you back to the era of tricorn hats, horse-drawn "ploughs," and water being hauled up in wooden buckets from "the strand."

The homes, shops, churches, and farms of Williamsburg are preserved and operated in the way they would have been in the eighteenth century.

Greene tends many landscapes that show the typical food of the day, which, of course, came mostly from the residents' own gardens, supplemented by neighboring farms with which they traded. It embodied the bartering environment from which modern locavore trends are taken.

Traditional Manure Hotbed

Greene told me that the earliest English gardening book he could find, *The Gardener's Labyrinth,* published in 1577, discusses the use of a hotbed. From extensive study of other gardening books published through the eighteenth century, he re-creates the method for starting spring food crops in the winter. The hotbed uses a base of manure, covered in soil, upon which the cold frame—which now would probably be called the hot frame—is placed.

As might be expected when you consider the era, building the old-style hotbed is a simple but labor-intensive practice. In Greene's 2012 book, *Vegetable Gardening the Colonial Williamsburg Way: 18th-Century Methods for Today's Organic Gardeners,* he shares historical methods of creating the hotbed and adds his analysis from re-creating the practice.

First, collect a good quantity of fresh manure, and pile it up to get the microbial activity working so it generates heat. Turn it once after six to ten days. Greene notes that horse manure gets hot enough, whereas cow dung does not. In the old days, they gathered fresh manure from the stables, which left it mixed with the horses' urine-soaked straw bedding. Today horse stalls are mostly bedded in sawdust, which would not combine with the manure to heat it up, so Greene recommends collecting manure from pastures. "This provides adequate heat for starting seedlings but does not maintain its heat for as long as a mix of manure and straw would."

He notes that a minimum amount of manure needed to make his hotbed, which is 10 feet long, would fill a pickup truck bed, so you must make friends with people running the local stables and be prepared to haul the manure yourself. As I said, it's a labor-intensive project.

Greene advises digging a trench for the hotbed and setting the frame on top of it. At Colonial Williamsburg, they have permanent pits lined with brick upon which the frames are set. The frames are 2 feet by 2 feet by 10 feet long, and two windows set at a steep angle cover the top. They

Wesley Greene adds manure to the pit of the hot bed in the Colonial Williamsburg historic garden. (Photo by Barbara Temple Lombardi, The Colonial Williamsburg Foundation)

start one hotbed in January for cool-season crops such as lettuce and cabbages and another one in March for hot-season crops such as cucumbers and tomatoes.

The steaming manure is shoveled into the trench and packed down in layers, because less air is better, allowing the manure to decay more slowly and radiate heat longer. Allow it to heat up for three or four more days, until the surface temperature is about 130°F.

Apply a layer of light soil 3–4 inches deep. Greene uses last year's fully composted manure. "This very light, porous soil mix allows the manure pile to breathe and continue to heat," he writes. The temperature drops to 100°F or so in a day and then to 70°F–80°F in a few more days.

When it reaches that temperature, seeds are planted and the glass tops are put on the frame. The soil is kept moist with tepid water during germination. In areas where snow and freezing weather are common, the walls of the frame need an external layer of insulation, and an insulating blanket is thrown over the glass at night. The top is vented every day, and care is taken not to let condensation build up on the inside of the glass and drip onto the bed. By April, Greene says, his robust vegetable starts are ready to plant into the garden.

Modern Adaptations to the Hotbed

With technology has naturally come a more modern way to use this practice. Today, gardeners can create a hotbed with the industrial equivalent of manure: the seed-starting heat mat. One method is to bury specially designed heating cables that are connected to a thermostat and radiate heat to keep the soil warm to a certain temperature. The other method is to extend heated water pipes into the ground under your garden, from a home heating system or a greenhouse. Heating coils or water pipes take the place of the manure and radiate heat upward into the soil.

The standard design for a hotbed with heating cables calls for burying them at least 6 inches below the soil level in a bed of gravel, layering 2 inches of soil on the cables, and protecting them with a tough, permeable barrier from being cut by garden tools. Cover the barrier with 6 inches of soil, into which you can start seeds, grow seedlings, or manage plants in pots. Just like the manure-based hotbed, this bed is covered by a frame, into which you put a thermostat with a soil-temperature probe, set for the ultimate temperature range for the plants you're growing.

Water-pipe-heated designs also are thermostatically controlled, and the pipes are set into the soil in a similar way.

With either design, you must be diligent in case the system fails. If electricity goes out or the boiler stops working, your cozy plants can soon be shivering and wilting, so you must have a backup plan to protect the plants, probably through layers of insulation on top of the plants and around the frame to help the bed retain heat as long as possible.

Using a Hotbed

Plants grown in this way, just as those grown in a greenhouse, are too delicate to withstand the vagaries of nature in its raw form. So if you're growing plants in a hotbed or hot frame, wean them off their comfortable environment and harden them slowly to the outdoor climate.

Another issue with plants in the ground above a hotbed is too much heat to the roots. Closer to the manure, cables, or pipes, the soil gets warmer and warmer, which limits the type of plants you can grow. Shallow-rooted lettuces are fine; root crops or deep-rooting vegetables are probably not.

Also, just as with greenhouse growing, you must be vigilant about watering and venting. The hotbed will dry out much faster than exposed soil, or even soil under a regular cold frame. If you've ever used a heat mat to start seedlings, you know how fast that soil can dry. So attend to watering and venting the plants on a daily basis.

Finally, the hotbed creates a climate that is much higher in humidity as well as heat, so seedlings are more susceptible to damping-off disease. That is another reason you must practice good growing techniques with careful watering, adequate plant spacing, and regular ventilation.

SPREAD OUT WITH GREENHOUSES AND POLYTUNNELS

A hotbed keeps plants warm, but its radiating heat won't do much for the gardener; instead, it is most tempting to imagine puttering around on winter days inside a warm greenhouse. You could be pruning the potted fruit trees brought inside, starting seeds early, getting another planting of short-season crops that wouldn't survive our cool, wet winter, or even growing hot-season crops such

Seattle Tilth has welcomed two generations of students to its iconic solar greenhouse.

as tomatoes! All that is possible, if you aren't in short supply of three key things: time, open land, and money.

Cold frames, and even cloches, can serve as miniature versions of an unheated greenhouse for starting plants or shielding tender perennials from harsh weather, but maybe that first small cold frame you prop up over the lettuce for a month in spring will be the gateway to supersizing those devices to have the luxurious effect of a walk-in structure. Installing a greenhouse might be the most important step home gardeners can take to advance their growing practices. This ultimate tool for cultivating your edible garden is certainly the last word in season extension.

High Tunnels or Polytunnels

American farmers and English gardening enthusiasts build large hoop houses—commonly called *high tunnels* in the United States and *polytunnels* across the pond—which have heavy greenhouse-grade plastic sheeting stretched tight over a tubular metal frame and a walk-in door on the end. These can be quite elaborate, with fans, heaters, and watering systems.

The prime US innovator in commercial hoop-house growing, Maine farmer Eliot Coleman, developed a mobile greenhouse of the high tunnel type, which moves from bed to bed seasonally on large tracks. Although it requires much more land than even a greenhouse, think of the possibilities. You'd have seasonal protection that could move from cool-tolerant plants to those that need it warm, and back again as needed. With savvy planning, you could also accomplish your crop rotation. That would truly be the dream of the ambitious gardener.

Greenhouses

Edible enthusiasts on a smaller property might choose to go with a traditional greenhouse, built more like a framed home and covered in a glazing

Farm-scale growing—or chicken keeping—is aided by a sturdy polytunnel. This one has walls that roll up for circulation.

Garden shows provide good greenhouse shopping.

A roomy propagation area inside Vern Nelson's greenhouse

material that lets through a lot of light. These, too, have been the product of innovation in the past few years, with new materials taking the place of traditional glass and wood. In the Northwest, a number of companies build and sell them commercially (see Resources), so all you have to do is provide a flat space of land for it to be set upon.

You can certainly build it yourself, and there are greenhouse kits and building plans available. Or you could seek some middle ground—cobbling together as many used windows and as much reusable framing lumber as possible and having a talented woodworker make you a one-of-a-kind structure. Veteran Portland garden writer Vern Nelson did that, erecting a surprisingly roomy greenhouse in the back corner of his city yard that charms the visitor with its eclectic mix of recycled styles.

Visiting the garden shows that sprout in our cities every spring will help you compress your greenhouse research because most of the regional manufacturers are in attendance. I've never owned one and only occasionally work in them, so to research greenhouses, I started at those shows. I followed that up with a visit to one of the larger homegrown operations, Charley's Greenhouse and Garden, a specialist in hobby greenhouses and accessories that has been in business for more than three decades. Based in Mount Vernon, Washington, Charley's provides gardeners across the United States with complete greenhouse kits in many sizes, but also parts, accessories, and unique devices such as environmental control units for do-it-yourselfers.

"Definitely there are more people interested in growing food in a greenhouse," says Carol

Yaw, co-owner with her husband, Charley, who founded the business in 1976, long before current innovations, such as high-tech, multilayered polycarbonate glazing, were invented. "Some people are choosing to grow all winter long, but others just lengthen their outdoor season by bringing their plants into the greenhouse in the fall and harvesting on, and starting earlier in the spring." Many home growers, she says, close up their greenhouse from November to February, possibly just using them to overwinter more delicate plants. But the possibilities abound. "You can overwinter many things with very little heat. People don't realize that," Yaw says. However, with a small heater or even just with double-walled glazing material, it's possible to grow cool-season crops, such as salad greens, radishes, leeks, herbs, and many more.

Four Levels of Warmth

There are four basic greenhouse climate zones that determine what you can grow based on temperature minimums:

- **Cold greenhouse:** with lowest nighttime temperatures of 35°F–45°F, it is suitable to overwinter many plants but not warm enough to actively grow most plants.
- **Cool greenhouse:** with lowest temperatures at 45°F–50°F, it is suitable to grow many cool-season leafy and root crops and winter-over plants wanting more warmth, such as lemons, limes, and grapes.
- **Moderate greenhouse:** with nighttime temperatures of 55°F–60°F, it is possible to grow warmer-season vegetables such as beans and cooler-tolerant tomatoes, along with strawberries and tree fruit.

- **Warm greenhouse:** with additional heat so the temperature doesn't drop below 65°F–70°F and extra lighting, it's no problem to grow peppers and tomatoes, and you can even grow melons, lemons, bananas, and many other crops.

Not surprisingly, many maritime Northwesterners are looking for help with their warm crops. "People from around here walk in every day and say, 'I need a greenhouse to grow tomatoes!'" Yaw says. Her response: "You need something with two layers that will insulate well. You're going to need some extra lighting if you want to grow year-round." As we talk, a compact, 250-watt metal halide light suspended on a track moves back and forth in their showroom greenhouse, beaming down light on a row of 3-foot-tall tomatoes sporting bright red fruit, ripening even in midspring.

Whether your budget allows for that holy grail or not, a greenhouse opens the door to a broader choice of plants and accelerates your success.

Solar-powered greenhouse vent opener

Size, Amenities, and Site

Size is an important consideration. "For most folks, 8-by-10-foot or 8-by-12-foot is an average size," she explains. If you're on a tight budget you might start with a 4-by-6-foot size, but that's just large enough to fit a couple of racks of seeds in, she says. "A 6-by-8-foot works if you have limited space and only want to start some seeds and winter-over a few plants." It's not uncommon for her to see serious gardeners opt for dimensions such as 14-by-20-foot, the size of a small commercial greenhouse.

A small hobby greenhouse generally consists of shelves along three walls. Most plants are grown in pots. Often some floor space is left open at one end of the greenhouse for taller potted plants.

The best orientation for the building is to run the long side east–west. If that's not possible, situate the greenhouse to make the most of the winter sun. The site should be protected from high winds and have good access to your home and garden. Good access to water and electricity is helpful too. Other considerations include:

- Along with size, consider shape and support. There are freestanding and home-attached types, with many forms and roof angles.
- A level base must be created for the greenhouse, with excellent drainage and a porous floor surface, which can be gravel, pavers, or other materials.
- Often the greenhouse frame is set on a solid, impervious surface such as paver blocks, engineered lumber, recycled plastic lumber, or a poured concrete footing.
- Framing material can be aluminum, wood, PVC pipe, or steel. Commonly used woods in the Northwest are western red cedar or redwood.

Crucial Question: Choice of Glazing

What you'll be doing with the greenhouse also dictates the type of covering, or glazing, materials. The two primary materials are traditional glass, commonly an $1/8$-inch, clear tempered safety glass, or the more recent innovation of rigid, multiwall polycarbonate. You also can find fiberglass, acrylic, vinyl, and polyethylene film coverings. Rigid multiwall polycarbonate has largely replaced the corrugated polycarbonate and flexible polyurethane of the old-style hoop houses. In the new material, which has been growing in use for the past five years or so, the layers are sandwiched together for more insulating value. Thicknesses range from $1/4$-inch (6 mm) twin-wall, $5/16$-inch (8 mm) three-wall, and $5/8$-inch (16 mm) three-wall and five-wall. With each increase in thickness, insulation value goes up and light transmission levels go down slightly. Here are some guidelines to choosing the glazing material:

- If you live in a mild climate and are just going to overwinter some potted plants and start seeds in the spring, glass might be best. You also could grow warm crops such as tomatoes and peppers in our climate, but you will need additional heat. In the summer, shading will be required, no matter what glazing material is used.
- If you live in a cold climate or one with harsh storms, multiwall polycarbonate is a better choice, both for the insulation factor and because it is less fragile. This is also the material of choice for people who want to grow plants year-round or for growing orchids, tropical plants, or other heat-loving plants. Some shading is recommended for this type of greenhouse also, but it will not get as warm as glass since some of the infrared, heat-inducing rays are reflected, making the interior temperature more stable.

What are the trade-offs between glass and polycarbonate? Glass is cheaper, offers the highest light transmission, and is showier. Polycarbonate is lighter weight and nearly unbreakable, as opposed to the brittleness of glass, and its insulating value means lower heating costs. It also diffuses the light for better plant growth.

Equipment

Greenhouse equipment can be very simple, with no lighting or electricity and just manual vents and a garden hose or drip irrigation system brought in from the garden. Too, there are solar-powered vent openers that open vents automatically as the temperature rises. But many people hire an electrician and plumber to make the greenhouse more functional. If you go that route, you might buy a ventilation system for better air circulation, adjustable lighting for seed-starting, and a mist system for humidity control. To control

the growing conditions, you need to know what they are, so a minimum-maximum thermometer, soil thermometer, humidity meter, light meter, and moisture meter are helpful.

COOL-SEASON KEYS TO LEARNING ADVANCED PRACTICES FOR SEASON EXTENSION

- Start earlier and grow later under a hoop house cloche.
- Provide solid protection with a cold frame.
- Combine a cloche or cold frame with a raised bed for even greater benefits.
- Grow year-round by using the ancient practice of hotbeds.
- Practice winter growing on a larger scale with a polytunnel or greenhouse.

9

Choosing Cool-Season Vegetables

When I stand amid my winter garden, sometimes the diversity amazes me. Spiky romaine lettuce heads, rosettes of forest-green spoon mustard, the shaggy mop of frisée endive, rows of frilly carrot tops and broad-leaf beets nestled deep in mulch—just the sight of them nourishes me nearly as much as eating them. Nothing brightens the winter landscape quite like rainbow chard, maroon kale, and purple broccoli. And when mustard greens sprout a waving crowd of yellow flowers, I know they are beckoning spring.

Diving deep into my garden journals and shelf of seed catalogs, here is a listing of cool-season vegetables commonly grown in the maritime Northwest, with some of my favorite varieties noted. This is not an exhaustive list; other varieties can be found at bioregional seed companies, and it is always good sport to see what local nurseries are carrying this season. When shopping, look for varieties specifically noted for cool-season growing, with language such as "short season," "early," or "good for winter."

Arugula—see *European Greens*

Asian Greens, Chinese Cabbages, and Mustard Greens

Brassica rapa spp.

Here on the Pacific Rim, we have an affinity for our neighbors across the ocean and have learned much about growing vegetables, especially the many flavors of hot and peppery greens, from Asian countries. Japan provides colorful mustard greens, and China has given us sturdy stir-fry leaves, to name just a few. Many of them are from the *Brassica* genus—an important point to

Arugula flower

Tatsoi

remember when planning crop rotation, because these are not immediately identifiable as kin to the heading cabbage or floreting broccoli.

Through the year I have found mustard greens to be one of my most reliable crops, nearly always in existence in some form. The broad leaves survive almost any cold snap once the plant has reached a few inches tall, and the plants may get to 3 feet tall before flowering, at which time their leaves are still tasty, as are the buds.

Spoon-shaped leaves, lined up prettily on the deep green rosette of the Tatsoi, which translates as "February vegetable," provide a succulent meal during the "hungry season" when the garden is just returning to life.

Pak choi and its cousin bok choi, the Chinese cabbages, provide large groupings of cupped leaves, while Mizuna delivers a Medusa-like mass of frilly green leaves. A variety of these leafy greens sprinkled in salads, soups, and stir-fry dishes adds zing to your food nearly year-round.

Spring or fall varieties: Red Giant mustard, Mizuna mustard, pak choi Chinese cabbage, Tatsoi (Tah Tsai) mustard, Komatsuna

Overwintering varieties: bok choi, Green-in-the-Snow mustard, Mizuna mustard, Osaka Purple mustard, pak choi Chinese cabbage, Tatsoi (Tah Tsai) mustard

Beans, Fava

Vicia faba

A sturdy stand of fava (or, more appropriately, *faba*) beans is a sure sign of successful overwintering. Favas are best grown in a stand rather than rows so they can support one another when their stalks get heavy with beans. A smaller-seeded variety is often used in cover crop mixes and grows well with small grains and clovers. As a legume, favas have the ability to "fix" atmospheric nitrogen onto their roots, which gets released back into the soil when they're cut down. If you grow the larger, flat-seeded variety and let it mature for eating, the leftover nitrogen is reduced, but you get a delicious crop.

Favas will amply reward the extra effort. Strip off a number of pods after they've plumped up, shell the green beans out of them, and cook them briefly in boiling water. Then slip the outer skin off each bean and finish cooking the soft green inner beans. My favorite recipe is to simmer them in

Broad Windsor fava bean harvest in June

olive oil with some green spring garlic and sprinkle the hot pile with sea salt.

Favas also have the benefit of sprouting in the cool soil of late fall, when most other plants are not able to do so. That means I can sow them into the beds after finally pulling out the last of a lingering summer or fall crop—a valuable feature, to be sure. If the plants reach even a few inches tall before the dark, rainy days of winter set in, they often survive the cold months and are among the first plants to take off for the sky in early spring. The taller plants can break under a snow load and can be more susceptible to cold, freezing after an abrupt temperature drop. But even then, I've had luck keeping some of them alive.

Once, after a particularly surprising cold night in early December, I surveyed my fava patch and found a number of brown, wilted plants . . . but not all were destroyed. So I quickly covered the whole patch with a double layer of floating row cover and watched the swaddled mass through the next few nights of icy cold. When it warmed and I could pull the FRC blanket off, I found the rest of the plants were fine, and in spring when they filled out, the stand was so abundant that I couldn't tell where the wilted ones had been.

Besides growing them over the winter, you also can plant these in early spring for a fall crop.

Varieties: Aquadulce, Broad Windsor

Beets

Beta vulgaris

One of the most reliable root crops in Northwest gardens, beets can be grown nearly year-round in the maritime climate. Their fairly short season of fifty to sixty days to mature roots means you can get at least two crops in the spring and another one in the fall. And while they're growing, snip leaves off the young plants to put in salads. When

Beets of all stripes and sizes

they're mature, both the tops and the roots can be eaten, although some varieties have tastier greens than others, and the older leaves of overwintered beets can be tough and tasteless.

Beets provide a colorful addition to the table, too. The roots can be gold, ruby, deep red, or even striped, in the case of Chioggia, which is sometimes called the "candy-cane beet" for its pink and white internal rings.

As with other roots, fall-planted or overwintering beets can be left in the soil, pretty much in cold storage through the cool seasons once they've reached maturity. Mulch them to the base of the leaves with straw, and they'll sit happily for many weeks. When growing in winter, thin to a larger 6-inch spacing, rather than the standard 4-inch spacing, so they have less competition for nutrients.

One of the few challenges with beets is the decimation of their leaves by the leaf miner, an energetic pest that also infects the leaves of Swiss chard and spinach, which share the family tree with beets. The best cultural control is to rotate crops religiously, but, unfortunately, that can limit the availability of these cool-season stars in many gardens. If the infestation is tolerable, choose beets over the other two because you can still eat the roots even if the leaves are attacked. Be sure to regularly pick off infected leaves and remove them from the garden.

Spring or fall varieties: Chioggia, Detroit Dark Red, Early Wonder Tall Top, Touchstone Gold

Overwintering varieties: Lutz, Winterkeeper

Broccoli

Brassica oleracea, **Botrytis group**

The many forms of broccoli provide abundant food, from the large-headed varieties in summer to the overwintering ones that send up only a small central head but follow it with long, voluminous sprouts sent out from the stem like a porcupine with its quills up. These purple sprouts, when cut and cooked like asparagus, are the stars of many a spring meal at my house. You can amaze friends and delight garden guests with the colorful, fractal-like sworls of the Romanesco variety, too. Its spiky, yellow-green head looks vastly different from the green heads of standard broccoli or the purple sprouts of winter.

Purple-sprouting broccoli

Because this cool-season plant germinates in cool soil but also can be started indoors and transplanted, it is one of the earliest crops for spring planting. A second crop can be planted midsummer for fall harvest, and the overwintering one makes this a nutrient-rich addition to the table for nearly three-quarters of the year. Along with the heads, sprouts, and florets, the leaves and spring buds and flowers of winter broccoli are also edible, and in fact quite delectable, making this plant a voluminous producer.

Spring or fall varieties: Calabrese, DeCicco, Green Sprouting, Romanesco, Thompson, Umpqua, Waltham (fall)

Overwintering varieties: Purple Sprouting

Broccoli Raab

Brassica rapa, **Revo group**

A graceful, easy-to-grow brassica that shares its name with broccoli but not its habit, broccoli raab is more like purple sprouting broccoli than the standard heading types. It is also called rapini, and there is a variety by that name. Varieties have different-sized leaves. From a small stand, you cut handfuls of long-stemmed shoots with light-green buds and eat the whole thing, stem to bud. Cook upright in an asparagus steamer or cut and sauté.

Varieties: Rapini, Sorrento, Zamboni

Brussels Sprouts

Brassica oleracea, **Gemmifera group**

A tall stalk of minicabbages is just what a person needs in midwinter, whether in Belgium or in Bellingham, so make this unique plant a part of your brassica rotation. As with the other large cole crops, they are hardy in our winter conditions, needing no help from season-extension devices if they are planted and tended on schedule. But with Brussels sprouts, there's the rub: Proper timing is essential to make them deliver sprouts. Calculating the planting date based on the variety's days to maturity is essential. You can begin to sow the longer-season ones in April and transplant them by mid-June.

The fuss and the wait is worth it, as you strip the stem clean with a paring knife and rush the little round gems into the kitchen for a midwinter's roasting or skillet sauté.

Varieties: Long Island Improved, Oliver Roodnerf, Rubine

Cabbage

Brassica oleracea, Capitata group

Generally, I think it's not a good idea to get a swollen head, as it often is accompanied by (a) an inflated sense of self or (b) a bad cold, but in the case of cabbage, it's delightful to see it happen.

My best cabbage experiences have always involved the overwintered types. Planted in late summer, the plants size up nicely and form their heads before the doldrums of winter hit. As with many brassicas, however, if a cold winter snap really settles in, you may be in for a bigger treat. The leaves of the cabbage head will get sweeter and crisper, and in some cases, the color will become ever more vibrant. The oblong heads of January King lived up to their name one year in my garden, becoming more and more regal as their leaves were enrobed in deepening purple veins through a snowy couple of weeks. Finally, I could handle the beauty no longer and began to cut and eat them.

As with Brussels sprouts, timing for sowing and transplanting cabbage is important. Make accurate calculations using the days to maturity and adjustments such as the fall factor and your own microclimate. But even in years when my calculations have been off or the weather has not plumped them to a regal degree, I've enjoyed the leaves of the vegetable in winter dishes.

Spring or fall varieties: Early Jersey Wakefield, Red Express, Danish Ballhead (fall), Stein's Late Flat Dutch (fall)

Overwintering varieties: January King

Brussels sprouts

January King cabbage

Carrots

Daucus carota

Spring carrots, pulled from the cool soil after having lived under a thick straw mulch through the winter, deliver a surprising sweetness along with the characteristic crunch. I love the earthy rootiness of carrots, and the orange spears deliver more vitamin A than any other vegetable (kale, another winter star, is a close second). But growing them over the winter would, I think, convert even a carrot dissenter. To a fan, eating a sweet spring carrot is like going to the World Series of carrotdom.

Growing techniques are similar to those for beets, although carrots won't jump out of the soil quite as consistently if sown too early. They like a well-draining, loose soil to send their roots down straight and true; they are just direct-sown, never transplanted, and need to be thinned for enough room to size up, especially in winter, when wider spacing is advisable. As with beets, I like to plant carrots in successive sowings a half-row at a time throughout each designated season, which gives a longer harvest. I increase that effect by varying the varieties, which have different days to maturity.

Get a faster start by presprouting the seeds (see the Helping Germination Along sidebar in chapter 6). Planting them under a cloche helps, too, but carrots need one extra bit of help: To avoid the dastardly carrot rust fly, which lays its eggs at the base of carrot seedlings, cover the carrots during germination and their first few inches of growth with well-secured floating row cover. The FRC prevents the adult fly from finding your carrots, and thus you will avoid the black tunnels that the boring larvae leave behind.

Spring or fall varieties: Bolero, Chantenay, Danvers Half Long, Dragon, Little Finger, Scarlet Nantes, Yaya (fall)

Overwintering varieties: Merida

Cauliflower

Brassica oleraceae, Botrytis group

The billowy white heads of cauliflower, nestled in a bowl of green leaves that serve to naturally blanch it, always look as light as clouds to me. Today you can grow more than just white cauliflower; there are yellow, orange, and even purple varieties—and a striking cross that has the pointed, fractal form of Romanesco broccoli—but I still prefer the chalky whiteness that seems to match the mild flavor and dense crunchiness.

Cauliflower is grown much like cabbage and broccoli, but more consistent results can be had by starting the seeds indoors and transplanting it. Take care to avoid stressing the plant, as that can result in stunted growth or small heads.

Spring or fall varieties: Shasta, Snow Crown, Veronica (Romaesco type—fall)

Overwintering varieties: Early Snowball

Celeriac

Apium graveolens, var. *rapceum*

Celeriac, although a close celery relative, is used very differently. It puts on a spray of leaves like parsley, then develops an edible root. It has a fussy habit similar to celery's (see below) and is nearly as challenging to grow. It will stand in the soil long into the fall.

Varieties: Brilliant

Celery

Apium graveolens, var. *dulce*

Tall, graceful bunches of celery stalks are a great addition to the herb section of the garden, but this is a challenging plant to grow. It's fussy and a heavy feeder, and timing is crucial. If you're successful, it should last well into late fall and even through winter, providing your own celery to use in the stuffing for the Thanksgiving turkey.

Veterans advise sowing this indoors in mid-spring and planting out with warm-season crops. It needs to be well watered, keeping its feet wet consistently as the stalks develop. It bolts and goes directly to seed if exposed to a period of very cool weather in the midst of a growing season. Moderating the climate with a cloche helps as the stalks develop; venting keeps it from growing too warm.

Varieties: Utah 52-70 Improved

Chinese Cabbage—see Asian Greens

Collards
Brassica oleracea, Acephala group

Broad, sturdy leaves of this plant, chopped and sautéed with onions, almost define the Southern cooking term "mess o' greens" to me, but collards seem to be an ideal cool-season plant. As with so many members of the *Brassica* clan, it sprouts in our long, cool spring, sails through a mild summer, and keeps producing long into the fall. Another planting in late summer provides an early spring supply to nearly round out the year with collards.

More consistent germination of this direct-sown crop can be assured by covering the bed with floating row cover after sowing, as the FRC keeps the seedbed moist longer. Allow to grow thickly, then eat the young leaves as you thin the plants. Collards are reliable and generally pest-free; the only problem I've encountered is sowing them too late in the fall, which results in an undersized winter crop that quickly bolts and goes to seed in the spring. But even that provides a silver lining, as the flower buds of the collard are as tasty as their cousins in the rest of the *Brassica* genus.

Spring or fall varieties: Georgia, Morris Heading, Vates

Overwintering varieties: Champion

Corn Salad—see *European Greens*

European Greens
Multiple genera and species

Our maritime Northwest climate is ideal for salad greens, and the mix of cultivated, heirloom, and wild plants that we can grow and eat in a salad is broad. Among the varied pickings, these are my favorites: nutty arugula (*Diplotaxis muralis*), whose leaves get hot and peppery with age; tender and mild corn salad (*Valerianella locusta*), which is edible right through its flower stage; and fine-leaved endive (*Cichorium endiva*), the easiest of the chicories. But there are so many more, from cultivated, savory sorrel (*Rumex scutatus*) or cress (*Lepidium sativum*) to abundant wild offerings such as purslane (*Portulaca oleracea* var. *sativa*) and miner's lettuce (*Claytonia perfoliata*), with which you can flavor a salad while weeding the beds for spring planting.

Corn salad (mache)

Spring or fall varieties: Arugula (Rocket): Sylvetta; Corn Salad (Mache): Vit; Endive: Tres Fine Maraichere, Rhodos; Sorrel: French; Cress; Miner's Lettuce; Purslane

Overwintering varieties: Arugula, Corn Salad, Miner's Lettuce, Purslane

Garlic

Allium sativum

Watching for the first shoots of garlic to poke through the mulch is my early-January garden entertainment, and just seeing them might bolster my immune system as much as eating garlic is reputed to do. I know we've reached the heart of our long spring when I cut the curly scapes off the top of my "hardneck" garlic to encourage the bulb to differentiate into cloves. Scapes are seed heads that are cut before the seed develops, and they are delicious in fresh spring garden dishes. Although softneck garlics do not put up this central seed head, they make up for it by being longer keepers after harvest.

Green garlic—the young bulbs dug up before the cloves have developed—also offer a milder garlic flavor. *Grow, Cook, Eat* author Willi Galloway of Portland suggests planting garlic much closer together than the ultimate spacing, then thinning the plants in the spring, pulling out every other one to get the young, green garlic while leaving room for the others to finish developing.

Garlic is planted in late October or November in our maritime climate, and the cloves seem oblivious to all but the most brutal winter weather. Even if a cold spell hits after they've sent up their first tender shoots, they'll often just replace that damaged first shoot with a fresh one when the weather warms. Harvest—starting in very late spring, about the last half of June—is dependent upon the variety. But that turns out to be perfect

Garlic with its curly "scapes," a spring delicacy

timing, because pulling this overwintered crop out of the garden as summer hits gives the maritime gardener a perfect space in which to begin the succession of fall plantings. Harvest when one-third of the leaves have yellowed, carefully forking up one plant to check its maturity before removing the whole stand.

Overwintering varieties: Hardneck: Chesnok Red, Music, German Red, Siberian, Spanish Roja; Softneck: Inchelium Red, Lorz Italian, Nookta Rose, Polish

Jerusalem Artichoke

Helianthus tuberosus

Productive, easy to grow, and tolerant of many conditions, Jerusalem artichoke is a tuber for our region. Not to be confused with the spiky, softball-sized flower heads of the artichoke, they share only a common name, and I've not detected any similarities in taste. Also called sunchoke or earth apple, Jerusalem artichoke is a member of the sunflower family. The pale green, pungent roots and tuberous stems grow in a mass below a well-mulched soil, and they are the epitome of earthiness when dug and scrubbed. They are very common in winter stews, probably because the plants are so prolific, but inform your guests, because the root can cause mild digestive problems in many eaters.

Plant in early spring in the same manner as potatoes, cutting tubers that have a few rooting "eyes" and sinking them 3–5 inches into the soil immediately after cutting. Harvest begins by early fall, and tubers can be stored in the ground through winter. They may become a perennial or regrow from previous planting spots, as it is difficult to remove all pieces at harvest.

Varieties: Mammoth French White

Kale

Brassica oleracea, Acephala group

Hands down the favorite winter green of maritime Northwest gardeners, the sturdy, long-lived kale can become miniature trees in our gardens as they offer long growth and harvest periods. In fact, I can only dimly recall a time when I didn't have some variety of kale standing in my garden. I generally take a break from growing it only if I run out of open bed space because of my rotation schedule. With the breadth and variety of brassicas available to us, this is sometimes a larger challenge than it would seem. But if you plan ahead and have enough space to move things around, a regular crop of kale should be high on your list of desirable cool-season vegetables.

Kale will sprout in the garden, but you can get a jump on the season by starting it very early indoors and transplanting. Then perform a later sowing outdoors that begins to produce in late spring and into the summer, and sow a third time in late summer for an overwintering supply. Snap larger leaves off the plant from the bottom up, and the plants soon resemble tree collards or very scraggly small trees—and, yet, just keep on growing. If a light frost hits them, so much the better; they shake off the rime and their taste becomes sweeter. When the biennial plant finally goes to flower in the end of its second season, eat the buds, too.

Kale is popular in winter soups, but I find it most delectable as a sturdy sauté, and you can feed it to the few non-kale lovers by chopping and quickly roasting it in a hot oven to make crispy, addictive kale chips.

Lacinato kale in snow

Spring or fall varieties: Russian Red, Dwarf Siberian, Lacinato (aka Dinosaur, Palm Tree, or Nero Di Toscana)

Overwintering varieties: Lacinato, Redbor, Siberian, Winterbor, Winter Red

Kohlrabi

Brassica oleracea, Gongylodes group

Perhaps this is the member of the *Brassica* clan that will get the most exclamations of surprise from visitors to your garden, as it is surely the most unusual to look at. A woody stem swells at the base to produce a rutabaga-shaped bulb with leaves exiting it at all angles. It has a mild flavor and can be eaten raw when young or peeled and cooked as it ages. As with most other brassicas, its leaves also can be eaten.

Kohlrabi has a fairly short season and can be planted early, so two spring crops are possible. Another crop for winter can be planted in early fall.

Varieties: Early Vienna

Leeks

Allium ampeloprasum

The staple of warming winter soups, leeks are long-season members of the onion family that form dense, cylindrical stems rather than bulbing roots. They can be slow to sprout if started from seed and must be started indoors unless the soil temperature is above 55°F. Broadcast into a flat, then carefully separate when transplanting. The young shoots are commonly laid in a trench, to which soil is added as they grow. That allows deeper planting and results in a larger part of the leek stem remaining white and tender for use. If transplanted by midspring, they will begin to produce in early fall but can stand in the garden well into winter, especially under a loose mulch. Successive sowings add to the harvest season.

Leek seedlings in a trench

Spring or fall varieties: Giant Caretan, Giant Musselburgh, Blue Solaise

Overwintering varieties: Giant Musselburgh, Blue Solaise, Scotland

Lettuce

Lactuca sativa

There is very little reason why a maritime Northwest gardener can't be eating lettuce out of the garden at least nine months of the year, the exceptions being August, December, and January. The myriad varieties include loose-leaf types from green to red, frilly to speckled; succulent or spiky rosettes of romaine types; single-serving, loose butterheads and larger cos heads; the crispheads; and the gourmet mesclun mixes that give you a selection of many "cut-and-come-again" types and may include European and wild greens. Browsing the lettuce pages in the seed catalogs, you quickly realize that it would take many seasons to munch your way through all the choices.

Begin your lettuce adventure by sowing seeds indoors in January, setting out the first crop under a cloche a few weeks afterward. Thomas Jefferson recommended that you sow a thimbleful of lettuce every week, which would certainly provide abundance for a large plantation and could be scaled back to a pinch weekly for a home garden. Winter and spring lettuce sowings can provide harvests from February through July, and summer sowings offer crops all through the fall, September through November (if covered).

The sowing progression needs to end only twice during the year: in late spring and in late fall. Lettuce sown to grow through the summer heat will be difficult, either tasteless or quick to bolt and go to seed. If sown too late in the fall, it won't have time to size up enough before winter hits and growth stops. But if fall-sown plants can get a

Three lettuces: Bronze Oak Leaf, Green Deer Tongue, and Forellenschluss

couple of sets of leaves and reach perhaps an inch in size, they will winter fine in a cold frame or a cloche (blanketed with an extra cover if bitter cold hits) and begin to grow as the days lengthen after the winter solstice.

Spring or fall varieties: Loose-leaf: Black-seeded Simpson, Red Sails, Merlot, Salad Bowl, Marvel of Four Seasons (also called Continuity), Red Oakleaf; Romaine: Forellenschluss, Green Deer Tongue, Little Gem, Winter Marvel; Butterhead: Buttercrunch, Marvel of Four Seasons, Speckles, Tom Thumb; Crisphead: Reine Des Glaces

Overwintering varieties: Little Gem, Marvel of Four Seasons, Rouge d'Hiver, Winter Density, Winter Marvel

Mustard Greens—see Asian Greens

Onions
Allium cepa

Whether you're growing a sweet onion to eat fresh on burgers, slender bunching ones for salads, the flattened Italian type to spear onto kebabs, or tough large ones to keep for winter use, all maritime Northwest gardeners should have some onions in the beds each year. You can grow them two ways: begin in early spring by sowing seeds indoors to plant out in midspring, or start in late summer to overwinter for transplanting. Spring-sown ones may be slow to sprout, but once up they are tough and easy to handle. When planting out, separate and lay in a trench, then backfill with soil. Late-summer sowings need to size up to chopstick width, then can be left in bunches to overwinter in the soil. They are dug up and transplanted to proper spacing in early spring.

Onions have a unique growth habit, beginning to bulb only when the day length is ideal. In the northern latitudes, we need to buy "long day" vari-eties, which are sometimes simply sold as north-ern types.

Bunching onions, also called scallions, form small bulbs but maintain green tops that also can be eaten. These are sown midspring to midsum-mer, with later sowings maturing in winter.

Spring or fall varieties: Copra, Redman, Red Zepplin, Ringmaster, Borrettana Cipollini, Walla Walla

Overwintering varieties: Evergreen bunch-ing, Copra, Ringmaster, Walla Walla

Parsnips
Pastinaca sativa

Vying with carrots for the prize as the sweetest root crop, parsnips are well suited to growth in the maritime Northwest garden. Their white or tan tapers get sweeter if exposed to frost, so a midspring planting of a variety with fairly long maturity yields roots in late fall and well into the winter. Like carrots, they can be mulched well and stored in the ground until needed.

Their cultivation is similar to carrots, although fussier: they are slow to emerge, sometimes taking three weeks or more. Factor that in when calculat-ing their days to maturity. Like carrots, they need a warmer soil to germinate, at least 55°F, so it is best not to plant them too early. Otherwise, get them started under a season-extension device. They have a reputation as fussy, weak seedlings that fail because they can't push through a crusty soil, so Territorial Seeds of Oregon offers the tip that "savvy old-timers sometimes plant radish seed in the furrow with parsnips to mark the rows and help break the soil surface for the slower-grow-ing parsnips." Parsnips also like a deeply dug bed of light soil so their roots can extend to their full length, which can be considerable. Cover the seed-

bed with floating row cover to deter the carrot rust fly, removing the cover only when the plants are a few inches tall.

If all that sounds like too much trouble, con-sider the mild, sweet taste you'll enjoy in midwin-ter stews, and take it as a challenge to add a row of parsnips to your winter garden.

Varieties: Cobham Improved Marrow, Gladia-tor, Harris Model

Peas
Pisum sativum

Peas are often the first spring vegetable to make an impression in my garden. As they haul themselves

Peas climb an A-frame trellis.

up the trellis, they affirm that my first growing season has arrived. It seems a torturous, long wait to begin eating the pods, but I often sow a quick-growing snow pea to get the season started and follow it up by a longer-maturing snap or shelling variety, and sow successively for a longer harvest season. If you just can't wait, that first, grassy taste of pea can be gained from some varieties that put on a lot of tendrils—cut and eat some of those.

However, winning the prize for early peas has been overshadowed by the less common practice of growing a second crop for the fall. That, I think, is where you can truly impress your friends and delight yourself with a taste that might seem out of season. But it's not: peas are eminently suitable as a fall crop. Planted in midsummer, kept well watered through the crucial sprouting stage, and carefully tended through the hottest weather, summer-grown peas reward you with a bountiful fall harvest. You can even get a jump on next spring's planting by sowing a crop of overwintering peas; those should be planted in early fall so they are 2–3 inches tall before winter; they may need some floating-row-cover protection from the harshest weather.

Coat the seeds with an inoculant when planting to increase the level of beneficial bacteria that help "fix" nitrogen on the roots of the plant and boost its growth. Look for "enation-resistant" varieties that help you avoid the pea enation virus, which can ruin a healthy plant by skeletonizing the leaves. Watch for aphid infestations on fall peas. Also, water plants from the base and provide good air circulation around them to minimize powdery mildew.

Spring or fall varieties: Shell: Alaska; Snap: Cascadia, Sugar Snap; Snow: Oregon Giant; Oregon Sugar Pod II

Overwintering varieties: Sugar Snap (frost resistant)

Radishes

Raphanus sativus

The round red radish of spring comes bob-bob-bobbing into the garden almost as early as the robins, and a row of cheery radish seedlings is a sure sign that the soil has warmed and dried enough to plant other early crops. Besides that duty, the spicy little roots quickly perk up a mellow salad or provide a happy-hour snack well salted and served alongside a hearty Northwest ale.

My favorite way to grow and eat radishes, though, is to ignore the roots. I like the winter radishes, like the old Black Spanish, which dates nearly to Colonial days. Sown in midsummer, it puts on a sturdy stand of leaves before winter hits, and in the spring the roots fill out, but the biennial plant also sends up its seed stalk, which is what I'm waiting for. The rangy white flower tops are edible, but leave them for the pollinators and wait for the seedpods to form. When young and tender, they are great tossed into salads, providing a light, tangy radish flavor. They also can be pickled. Rattailed radishes also are grown for their pods, which are longer.

Radishes are quick-growing and ideal for succession sowing to get a long harvest. They should be picked as soon as they size up, because they can quickly become woody, and the tops of the roots, sitting above the soil, are susceptible to slug damage. Daikon, a giant Asian type, is sown in midsummer for a fall crop, and a second crop of the small radishes may be sown in late summer as well.

Spring or fall varieties: Champion, Cherry Belle, Easter Egg, French Breakfast

Overwintering varieties: Black Spanish, Minowase Daikon, Rattailed

Rutabaga

Brassica napus

A star of the winter root crops, rutabaga produces a large, bulbous root that stores well in the ground in our maritime Northwest climate and offers food by the pound. It is actually a cross between a turnip and a cabbage, with a mild flavor well suited as a base to a winter stew when cubed, or it can be cooked and mashed like potatoes. It's often called winter turnip or Swede. Plant it in late spring for a fall crop that can be mulched and held in the garden bed until needed.

Varieties: Marian

Salsify

Tragopogon porrifolius

An old perennial vegetable that is experiencing a resurgence of interest, salsify will surely be among the most unusual things you grow. According to Seed Savers Exchange, it is also called "vegetable oyster" for its roots bearing a striking resemblance to oyster in flavor. Plant in midspring for roots that mature in fall and can be mulched and stored in the soil. But you can also eat its grasslike leaves and, if overwintered to grow a second year, cut off its new growing shoots in the spring. Let its tall, purple, asterlike flowers develop and enjoy those— or eat the buds. The slender root develops like a turnip, needing light, deeply worked soil. It comes out brown and hairy, but peel it to reveal a snowy white interior.

Varieties: Mammoth Sandwich Island

Shallots

Allium cepa, **Aggregatum Group**

The sweet, rich flavor of shallots are a garden treat not to be missed. A more delicate, cultivated member of the onion family, shallots are grown in the same way as garlic, although they develop a bit differently. One shallot bulb does not produce a head but, rather, a loosely connected bunch, which sends up a grassy head of shoots.

Plant in a shallow bed of loose, well-draining soil in October. Planting too deeply can cause the bulb to rot. Harvest in a similar way to garlic: Begin checking plants for maturity when the tops yellow and die back. Use small bulblets around the larger bulbs first, drying and storing the bulbs as you would onions and saving the best specimens for seed as next year's crop.

Varieties: Dutch Yellow, French, Holland Red

Sorrel—see *European Greens*

Spinach

Spinacia oleracea

The sturdy leaves of spinach are well adapted to the maritime Northwest climate. In fact, our region produces a majority of the commercial spinach and seed. The plant is particularly suited to our cool weather and can be planted for spring, fall, and winter crops.

Plant in midspring under season-extension devices, when the soil has reached 55°F. It might be challenging to keep the seedbed moist during the germination period, which can be as long as three weeks. Late-summer plantings for fall sprout more quickly, but similar care must be taken to keep the seeds well watered. If planted too late in the spring and young plants experience warm weather, many varieties quickly bolt. Winter plantings should be given wider spacing for best air circulation to avoid downy mildew. Yellowed or mildewed leaves should be removed from the garden and discarded.

Note: Some leafy greens from other families are called spinach because they have a similar flavor. New Zealand spinach (*Tetragonia expansa*) is a vigorous, ground-cover-like plant that grows through the summer. Perpetual spinach (*Beta vulgaris* var. *cicla*) is actually from the beet family and is a type of chard that also produces spinach-flavored leaves over a long season.

Spring or fall varieties: Bloomsdale, Olympia, Samish, Teton, Tyee

Overwintering varieties: Giant Winter, Tyee, Winter Bloomsdale (or Bloomsdale Long-Standing)

Swiss Chard
Beta vulgaris

Glossy upright leaves of chard, or "leaf beet," as it used to be known, grace many maritime Northwest vegetable gardens throughout the winter. Chard differs from beets in that it does not make a bulbing root. The flat, slightly cupping midribs

Sturdy Swiss chard provides a bountiful harvest.

Edible Flowers and Herbs for the Cool-Season Garden

Brighten up salads with hardy flowers and spice up cooking with the leaves of herbs that grow abundantly in the Cool-season garden. Snip flower heads when they are at their brightest for the best flavor. I always let a few go to seed so the plants will work their way around the garden. Some, like calendula and Johnny jump-up, can "self-sow" thickly enough to become a winter cover crop. Here are some favorites:

Borage
Calendula
Chives
Cilantro
Dandelion
Johnny jump-up
Parsley

---

come in a variety of colors and are juicy and crunchy, needing a bit more cooking time than the leaves. Begin sowing in early spring, and easily get two crops or a continual harvest until summer. Pick up sowing for fall and winter as soon as the summer heat fades. Plants can be reduced to just a couple of leaves and will regrow, although subsequent crops may not be as vigorous. Chard can stand in the garden through winter weather that includes snow or periodic freezing. If a hard freeze wilts the leaves, it may sprout new ones in early spring.

Chard is susceptible to the leaf miner and should be rotated regularly into different beds that have not had other beet family plants, to minimize the pest problem. Pick off and destroy affected leaves.

Spring or fall varieties: Bright Lights (also called Five-Colored Silverbeet), Golden, Perpetual, Rhubarb

Overwintering varieties: many will overwinter, but Fordhook Giant is a star

Turnips

Brassica rapa, **Rapifera group**

Smaller cousin to the rutabaga, the turnip is one of the oldest crops grown in the United States. Both the greens and the round roots can be eaten. With a much shorter season than the rutabaga, turnips are often sown in midspring for harvest by the height of summer. Cover with floating row cover to protect the seedlings from flies that lay eggs that hatch into root maggots. Turnips are best picked in cool weather just as they mature, to avoid damage from the pest, which can burrow through and destroy the root. Also, turnip greens often are picked and stewed as an alternative to eating the root.

Varieties: Golden Ball, Purple Top, White Globe

COOL-SEASON CROPS

Growing vegetables year-round requires planning on when to sow, how long the crop will grow, and if or when it will need help from season-extension techniques. See notes 1–4 on page 154 for chart explanations.

CROP	GERMINATION/ GROWING DEGREE DAY BASE TEMPERATURE–MINIMUM	GROWING TEMPERATURE–OPTIMAL	HOLDING TEMPERATURE (IN GROUND STORAGE)–MINIMUM	SOW OR TRANSPLANT PERIODS[1]	DAYS TO EMERGENCE	TYPICAL DAYS TO BEGIN HARVEST[2]	GROWING SEASON[3]	SEASON-EXTENSION TECHNIQUES[4] & SEASONS TO USE THEM
Arugula (European Greens)	40°F	60°F–65°F	15°F	Feb.–May, Aug.–Sept. (fall & OW)	2–15	30–50 S	1–7	
Asian Greens: Bok Choi & similar	40°F	60°F–65°F	20°F	Feb.–May, Aug.–Sept. (fall & OW)	2–15	30–50 S	1–3, 5	FRC–6 CL–7
Beans, Fava	40°F	60°F–65°F	15°F	*Feb.–Apr., Oct.–mid-Nov. (OW)	8–18	70–180 S	1, 2, 6, 7	
Beets	40°F	60°F–65°F	15°F	*Feb.–May, July–mid-Oct. (fall & OW)	7–10	60–70 S	1–3, 5	FRC–1 CL–1 SM–7
Broccoli	40°F	60°F–65°F	10°F	Feb.–May, mid-July–mid-Sept.	5–17	55–85 S	1–3, 5–7	FRC–1
Broccoli Raab	40°F	60°F–65°F	10°F	Feb.–May, Aug.–mid-Sept.	5–17	40–85 S	1–3, 5–7	FRC–1
Broccoli—sprouting	40°F	60°F–65°F	10°F	June–July (OW)	5–17	220–250 S	4–2 OW	
Brussels Sprouts	40°F	60°F–65°F	10°F	June–July (OW)	5–17	80–160 T	4–7	
Cabbage—early (summer-fall)	40°F	60°F–65°F	10°F	Apr.–May	5–17	50–70 T	1–3	FRC–2
Cabbage—late (winter)	40°F	60°F–65°F	10°F	mid-May–mid-July (OW)	5–17	85–220 T	4–7	
Carrots	38°F	60°F–65°F	15°F	*Mar.–May, mid-Sept.–mid-Oct. (OW)	6–21	55–75 S	2–5	FRC–2, 5 SM–7

CROP	GERMINATION/ GROWING DEGREE DAY BASE TEMPERATURE–MINIMUM	GROWING TEMPERATURE–OPTIMAL	HOLDING TEMPERATURE (IN GROUND STORAGE)–MINIMUM	SOW OR TRANSPLANT PERIODS[1]	DAYS TO EMERGENCE	TYPICAL DAYS TO BEGIN HARVEST[2]	GROWING SEASON[3]	SEASON-EXTENSION TECHNIQUES[4] & SEASONS TO USE THEM
Cauliflower	45°F	60°F–65°F	10°F	Feb.–May, mid-July–mid-Sept.	5–17	60–100 T	2–6	FRC–2
Celeriac and Celery	55°F	60°F–70°F	10°F	Feb.–Mar.	7–20	85–120 T	1–4	CL–1
Chinese Cabbage (Asian Greens)	45°F	60°F–65°F	10°F	Feb.–Mar., June–July (OW)	5–15	75–80 S	1–3, 5, 6	CL–1
Collards	40°F	60°F–65°F	10°F	Mar.–Apr., mid-May–mid-July (fall & OW)	5–17	55–60 S	1–7	
Corn Salad (European Greens)	40°F	60°F–65°F	0°F	Feb.–May, Aug.–Sept. (fall & OW)	2–15	50 S	1–7	
Cress (European Greens)	40°F	60°F–65°F	15°F	Feb.–May, Aug.–Sept. (fall & OW)	2–15	15–60 S	1–3, 5, 6	
Endive/Chicory (European Greens)	45°F	60°F–65°F	10°F	Feb.–May, Aug.–Sept. (fall & OW)	2–15	65–85 S	1–3, 5, 6	CL–1
Garlic (cloves)	45°F	55°F–75°F	0°F	*late Oct. (OW)	n/a	250–270 S	6–3 OW	SM–7
Jerusalem Artichoke	45°F	60°F–65°F	0°F	July–Aug. (OW)	n/a	100–105 S	6–3 OW	
Kale	40°F	60°F–65°F	0°F	Feb.–May, mid-July–mid-Sept. (fall & OW)	5–17	60 S	1–3, 5–7	FRC–1
Kohlrabi	40°F	60°F–65°F	15°F	mid-July–mid-Aug.	5–17	105–110 S	7–3 OW	
Leeks	45°F	55°F–75°F	0°F	Mar.–May, Aug.–Sept. (fall & OW)	6–16	30–75 T	2–5	SM–7

CROP	GERMINATION/ GROWING DEGREE DAY BASE TEMPERATURE–MINIMUM	GROWING TEMPERATURE–OPTIMAL	HOLDING TEMPERA-TURE (IN GROUND STORAGE)–MINIMUM	SOW OR TRANSPLANT PERIODS[1]	DAYS TO EMERGENCE	TYPICAL DAYS TO BEGIN HARVEST[2]	GROWING SEASON[3]	SEASON- EXTENSION TECHNIQUES[4] & SEASONS TO USE THEM
Lettuce	40°F	60°F–65°F	15°F	Feb.–May, Aug.–Sept. (fall & OW)	2–15	30–50 S	1–7	FRC–1, 5 CL–6 CF–7
Mustard Greens (Asian Greens)	40°F	60°F–65°F	20°F	Feb.–May, Aug.–Sept. (fall & OW)	2–15	30–50 S	1–7	FRC–1
Onions (bulb)	45°F	55°F–75°F	0°F	Jan.–Mar., late Aug.– early Sept. (OW)	n/a	50–110 T	1–5	SM–7
Onions (scallions)	45°F	55°F–75°F	0°F	mid–Apr.–May, mid–July–Aug.	6–16	80–90 S	2–4	
Parsnips	40°F	60°F–65°F	0°F	*Mar.–mid-July (OW)	15–25	110–120 S	2–5	FRC–2 SM–7
Peas	40°F	60°F–65°F	20°F	Feb.–May, Aug.–Sept. (fall & OW)	6–14	55–75 S, 90 S fall, 180 OW	1–3, 5, 6	FRC–1
Radishes	40°F	60°F–65°F	0°F	*Feb.–May, Aug.– Sept. (fall & OW)	4–11	20–35 S, 200 OW	1, 2, 4–3 OW	
Rutabaga	40°F	60°F–65°F	0°F	*Apr.–May, July (OW)	5–17	85–95 S	3, 4, 4–1 OW	FRC–3 SM–7
Salsify	45°F	55°F–75°F	0°F	Mar.–May	5–15	110–150 T	3–6	
Shallots (bulb)	45°F	55°F–75°F	0°F	*late Oct. (OW)	n/a	120–180 S OW	6–3 OW	SM–7

CROP	GERMINATION/ GROWING DEGREE DAY BASE TEMPERATURE—MINIMUM	GROWING TEMPERATURE—OPTIMAL	HOLDING TEMPERA- TURE (IN GROUND STORAGE)—MINIMUM	SOW OR TRANSPLANT PERIODS[1]	DAYS TO EMERGENCE	TYPICAL DAYS TO BEGIN HARVEST[2]	GROWING SEASON[3]	SEASON- EXTENSION TECHNIQUES[4] & SEASONS TO USE THEM
Sorrel (European Greens)	40°F	60°F–65°F	15°F	Feb.–June	2–15	60 S	1–4	
Spinach	40°F	60°F–65°F	0°F	Apr.–May, late Aug.– early Sept. (fall & OW)	6–21	30–50 S, 180 OW	1–3, 5–1 OW	FRC–5 SM–7
Swiss Chard	40°F	60°F–65°F	10°F	Feb.–May, July–Sept. (fall & OW)	5–17	50–60 S	1–7	
Turnips	40°F	60°F–65°F	10°F	*Apr.–May, June–July (OW)	5–17	45–65 S, 180 OW	2, 3, 4–2 OW	FRC–2 SM–7

(1) See germination temperature to determine whether to sow outdoors or in pots. For listings with *, sow seeds in bed only, no transplanting. Overwintering (OW) plants may be started in pots (except *) if necessary for succession planting after summer crops.

(2) Days to harvest are from sowing date (S) or transplant date (T). For crops sown into an overwintering period (OW), days to harvest may be greatly extended due to the fall factor and dormant periods. See chapter 6 for details.

(3) Seasons: 1 = early spring; 2 = midspring; 3 = late spring; 4 = summer; 5 = early fall; 6 = late fall; 7 = winter. See chapter 6 for complete descriptions.

(4) Season-extension techniques: straw mulch (SM); floating row cover (FRC); cloche (CL); cold frame (CF). See chapters 4, 7, and 8 for details.

Sources: *Washington State University Master Gardener Manual,* Oregon State University, Territorial Seed Company, *Knott's Handbook for Vegetable Growers,* personal experience

10

Troubleshooting

In the cool-season garden, common challenges can arise from pests and diseases and can be caused or made worse by the gardener's inattention or sloppy cultural practices. My first defense is always to practice sound cultural techniques to keep the plants and garden environment healthy. When pests or diseases do appear, my first step is to identify the problem and take the least toxic, most sustainable approach possible—the first stages of integrated pest management (IPM). Although I understand that pesticides are sometimes necessary as a last resort and can be applied safely, I do not use them, so cannot offer that type of advice.

Below is a primer on good cultural practices, followed by a list of common pests and diseases seen on cool-season plants in the maritime Northwest garden. Brief descriptions and nontoxic control methods are included, but readers are encouraged to seek in-depth help through the Resources listed at the back of this book.

CULTURAL PRACTICES FOR GARDEN HEALTH

In general, a vegetable garden remains relatively healthy if a few sound cultural techniques are regularly practiced. These include crop rotation; polyculture; good watering, air circulation, and sanitation practices; and consistent observation and early management when problems appear.

Air circulation is a key to minimizing diseases, because it helps dry out the plants. Even if you are careful with watering, rain and dew envelop our plants during the cool seasons and evaporate very slowly. Pruning vining plants on a trellis can ensure good air circulation, for instance, and keeping the lower leaves or branches from touching the soil helps. Wider spacing of winter-grown plants also enhances air movement. Regular picking of mature leafy greens allows air through the plants and reduces chances of rot, too.

Crop rotation, discussed in chapter 4, is practiced for a number of reasons, but a primary one is to keep down disease and pest populations. Particular plant families are susceptible to certain problems, which tend to build up over time if given the chance. Planting crops from the same

Getting Expert Help

This chapter only scratches the surface of potential problems and solutions and does not provide methods for identifying the problem with your plant. Expert help is available from online databases, university-sponsored consulting programs, and a host of great books.

Your first step might be to take a segment of an affected plant, or a sample of a pest, to the local Master Gardeners. This is a group of university-supported volunteers that operates in many communities. Master Gardeners hold regular clinic hours at farmers markets, big-box home stores, and many other locations. They're easily found through an Internet search.

The county extension office, operated by a land-grant university, is another great resource. In many places, extension agents who are experts in horticulture or pest management provide free advice to a gardener grappling with an unknown problem.

Extensive online databases, usually created by universities, can be consulted for pictures of plant diseases and pests and advice on how to treat the problem. Always look for a reputable organization behind the online resource to make sure the advice you get is scientifically sound and is safe for you, your children, your pets, and the environment.

Excellent books help you do your own research and sleuth out the problem. See the Resources list in the back of this book.

family in the same location in your garden season after season gives that pest or disease a chance to build up its population, because you consistently provide it with its favorite food. Therefore, break the cycle by rotating plants from other families into that bed. A three-year rotation is commonly advised to reduce pest and disease populations to a manageable level.

Garden sanitation means getting rid of the pests or disease organisms when you see them. It's as simple as plucking destructive worms and slugs off your plants, pinching off diseased or pest-damaged leaves, and promptly removing them and other affected plant material from the garden. Because most home composting systems do not heat the compost to a high enough temperature to kill disease organisms, it's best to discard diseased plant material in the garbage or municipal yard-waste bins.

Polyculture is a fancy word for planting a variety of things all jumbled together in your garden. Variety provides food and habitat for beneficial insects, which often are your best defense against pests. Polyculture offers the gardener many food choices, too, if one crop happens to be ravaged by a pest or disease infestation. Growing many things

Misters work well for seedlings

chance of it developing by keeping
only lightly moist, providing good air
and starting seeds with a heat mat or
atly warm room. Do not reuse soil
nce of damping off disease.

ildew, evidenced by fuzzy white
underside of leaves, can cause yellow
ts on leaf surfaces, which then curl or
ostly evident on beets and spinach.
ed by consistently moist conditions,
cool weather or on overwintered
res in the soil near plants where it's
id overhead watering, pick off and
ed leaves, and rotate crops.

t is a fungus that causes yellowing
which then turn brown and dry, and
es on stems. It can spread quickly to
ant, and it will remain in the soil. It
only seen on tomatoes but also can

affect potatoes. Prune off and destroy affected material, provide good air circulation, avoid overhead watering, and rotate crops.

Pea enation mosaic virus, spread by aphids, can cause mottling and distortion of the leaves and a brown stain on the pea berries (seeds in the pod). Buy enation-resistant varieties, remove and destroy affected plant material, and control aphids.

Powdery mildew, a fungal disease that begins as spots on the leaves and progresses to a white or gray covering over the leaves and stems, commonly affects peas and squashes. It is spread by moisture, so avoid overhead watering and promote good air circulation. It also spreads faster in warm, humid conditions, so take particular care with fall peas, keeping them away from squashes; grow varieties known to be resistant. Remove affected material and rotate crops.

means you have more chance to rotate crops, which better uses the entire spectrum of soil nutrients, so plants don't become stressed because of an overdepletion of some element essential for their growth. That also means you can use less fertilizer.

Watering practices go a long way toward keeping common cool-season diseases at bay. Some of our biggest problems, such as late blight or powdery mildew, are triggered by moisture that sits on leaves and stems over a long period of cool weather, when evaporation occurs very slowly. If you use a drip irrigation system or another method to water at the soil level and keep moisture off the plants as much as possible, you reduce the chance for bacteria or fungi to take hold. Consistent watering is also an element of control, because deep, regular watering results in healthier plants and a more active soil food web, both of which are front lines of defense against diseases.

PESTS

I think gardeners should tolerate a bit of plant damage from the other creatures that inhabit the garden, but when something goes from nibbler to pest, it's time to take action. Sometimes prevention is the best defense, while other critters just need to be hunted with a flashlight and bucket of soapy water.

Aphids, tiny green, gray, or black sucking insects of various species, usually are seen in masses on stems or underside of leaves. Feeding on the sap of a plant, they can cause wilting and browning of leaves and stems and leave behind a sticky substance. Ladybugs and other beneficial insects are great predators. Destroy aphids by hand or use a hard spray of water to wash aphids off the plant, repeated within a few days. Also, prune off badly infested or destroyed areas.

Carrot rust fly (*Psila rosae*), a shiny black fly with an orange head, lays eggs in the soil at the base of carrots and parsnips. When eggs hatch, white maggots burrow through roots, leaving behind a rust-colored frass (bug poop). Discolored sections may be cut out of roots but can extensively damage or render them inedible. Divert this pest by covering carrot and parsnip seedbeds with floating row cover, leaving the cover on the bed until the plants are 3–4 inches tall.

Cabbage looper (*Trichoplusia ni*), a pale green worm that develops a white stripe as it matures, crawls by arching its body into a loop. Adults are brown moths with forewing spots. They deposit eggs on foliage and pupate on the underside of leaves. Larvae are day feeders that chew holes in the leaves of many cabbage-family plants, including broccoli and kale. Covering young plants with floating row cover can prevent the moths from laying eggs on leaves. Hand-pick loopers and destroy eggs.

Cabbage maggot (*Delia radicum*) is a burrowing soil maggot that digs into the roots of many members of the cabbage family and can do much damage. As with the carrot rust fly, it is the result of a fly that lays its eggs at the base of the plant. White maggots feed on the roots before going into their pupa stage and then emerging as flies. There are three or four cycles per year. In early spring, the first flies emerge before predators such as beetles are out, so it's up to gardeners to protect their young brassicas. Most effective is to blanket the seedlings with floating row cover, making sure that it is well sealed to prevent entry. I like to dig a trench around the bed and bury the edges of the FRC.

Imported cabbage worm (*Pieris rapae*), also known as the cabbage butterfly, is the common white butterfly with black wing spots that we see spastically cavorting through our brassicas. While it may seem harmless, it's laying eggs on the underside of the leaves. Groups of tiny white or yellow eggs can be found and should be destroyed. If not, they hatch into a ½-inch green worm, which feeds on the leaves and will eventually pupate into that butterfly. Pick and destroy the eggs and the worms. Catch the butterfly if you can. Cover young brassica plants with floating row cover to prevent the eggs from being laid.

Cutworm is a generic name for a number of different species of pest that typically have a soil-dwelling worm stage followed by an adult moth stage. They are sometimes called "millers." Often they feed on shoots of young plants but also can emerge to feed on the stems and leaves as well. Many are nocturnal feeders, so go out at night with a flashlight to pick them off and destroy.

Spinach leaf miner (*Pegomya hyoscyami*), which feeds on beets and Swiss chard as well as spinach, is a common problem in maritime Northwest vegetable gardens. Smallish flies lay masses of white eggs on the underside of leaves. When they hatch, the pupae tunnel into the leaf and leave sunken, gray trails as they mine through the leaf cells. Regularly check for eggs and hand-crush

Snails seek the underside of pot rims.

them, and remove any affected leaves. Reduce the presence of the host plant by rotating crops.

Slugs and snails, two species of gastropods that feed at night and live in moist corners of the garden, are the most common pests on maritime Northwest vegetables. Hunt with a flashlight, pick, and destroy. Attract and trap slugs and snails by laying a board in the garden to which they can attach, or make a beer trap with a plastic container sunk partly into the soil. Protect young plants with a barrier of copper strips.

Whitefly (*Trialeurodes vaporariorum*) is commonly found in greenhouses, a product of a warm environment and lack of natural predators. The small white flies lay eggs on leaves; the eggs hatch into sucking insects. They can be a problem on seedlings grown indoors to larger size or on vegetables grown in a greenhouse. White flies attack plants worst that are stressed from lack of watering, so regular watering is a good defense. Also, getting the plants outside to air them, allowing beneficial insects into the greenhouse, scrubbing the larvae off their leaves, and vacuuming up or setting sticky traps for the flies can help.

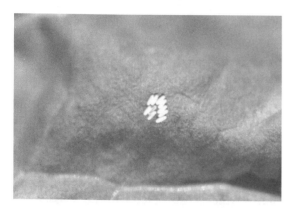

Leaf miner eggs on a chard leaf

Damping off can be seen at the base of the stem in the front seedling.

DISEASES

While a cool-season climate allows an abundance of growing, it also fosters some plant diseases that can really take hold and decimate our most beloved crops. Crop rotation is the most common remedy for fungal and bacterial diseases that can live in the soil, and good watering and sanitation practices also help.

Anthracnose, sometimes called "shot-hole" because of the multiple round holes it produces on leaves, is a fungal disease commonly affecting lettuce. It is triggered by water spots, which become holes with black edges. It quickly kills the leaf and moves to others. Remove affected material, water only at the base of the plants, and rotate crops.

Powdery mildew on a to...

Black rot, a bact... many brassicas, firs... the leaves, which al... their veins. Leaves... can appear on the s... and is spread by wa... remove affected pl... rotate crops.

Club root, a fu... sicas, can stunt or... soil unusable for a... family for many ye... ules or deformatio... even radishes and... soil. It also prefers... ing these crops in... pH, removing dis... At least a six-year... root is detected.

Damping off,... destroys seeds as... newly emerged s... rot or seedling st... It is made worse...

Minim... seedbe... circula... in a co... that ha...

Dow... spots o... or brow... wither. ... It can be... especial... plants, a... detected... destroy a...

**Late ... of the lea... brown bl... destroy th... is most c...

Appendix: Building Projects

COMBINED RAISED BED AND COLD FRAME

These plans are for a 30-inch by 60-inch combined raised bed and cold-frame box. Both are made of wood, and the cold frame is sheathed in plywood and topped with a transparent lid, which can be propped open in two positions. The lid can be made of rigid polycarbonate, acrylic, Plexiglas, et cetera.

Adjust the size of the bed and cold frame to fit your available space or salvaged window sashes for the cold frame top.

Materials

- 2x6 lumber, in quantity (see Cutting Instructions)
- 2x4 lumber, in quantity (see Cutting Instructions)
- 2x2 lumber, in quantity (see Cutting Instructions)
- Plywood, in quantity (see Cutting Instructions)
- 1-inch-square hardwood stock, 2 @ 28 inches
- Transparent material for cold frame top, 59 inches x 30¾ inches
- 3-inch wood screws, in quantity
- 1¾-inch wood screws, in quantity
- 1-inch washered screws, in quantity
- 4-inch hinges, 2
- ¼-inch x 2½-inch bolts, 8, with washers and wingnuts

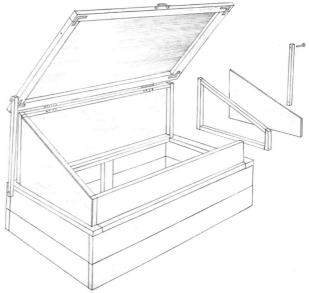

- ¼-inch x 3-inch bolts, 2, with 4 washers and 4 nuts
- ¼-inch x 4-inch eye bolts, 2
- 6-inch L brackets, 4
- 5-inch handle, with bolts, washers, and nuts

The Raised Bed

This is a simple rectangular box, with two levels pinned together. It would take two cubic yards of soil to fill it to 10 inches deep. Use a lower soil level to allow more "head height" for the plants to grow taller under the cold frame.

Cutting Instructions

- 2x6 front and back wall pieces: (A) 4 @ 60 inches
- 2x6 end pieces: (B) 4 @ 27 inches
- 2x4 lateral supports: (C) 2 @ 20 inches
- 2x4 caps: (D) 2 @ 57 inches; (E) 2 @ 30 inches

Building Instructions

1. Using 3-inch wood screws, attach two A and two B 2x6 pieces to make a box. Set it on the garden bed and make sure it is level and square. Build a second box with the remaining A and B pieces, then stack it on top of the first box. Using 3-inch screws, pin the boxes together with supports C, centered on the front and back walls, as shown.

2. Using 3-inch screws, attach the 2x4 cap pieces D and E flush with the outer edge of the box. Fill the raised bed with soil.

The Cold Frame

Now that the sturdy raised bed is in place, build the cold frame. It will sit on the raised bed cap. Build each wall frame, then assemble with screws. This allows for easy disassembly and storage, extending the life of the cold frame.

Cutting Instructions

- 2x6 front wall: 54 inches
- 2x2 left and right side-wall frames: (F) 2 @ 18 inches; (G) 2 @ 6 3/16 inches; (H) 2 @ 26¼ inches; (J) 2 @ 23 inches
- 2x2 back-wall frame: (K) 2 @ 54 inches; (L) 2 @ 18 inches
- 2x4 lid frame: (M) 1 @ 60 inches (back); (N) 2 @ 26⅞ inches (ends)
- 2x2 lid frame: (O) 1 @ 60 inches (front)
- Plywood back wall: 57 inches x 18 inches
- Plywood side walls: 23½ inches x 23½ inches, cut in two as shown
- Clear top: 59 inches x 30¾ inches

Building and Operating Instructions

1. Cut a piece of plywood 23½ inches square. Mark

Steps 1 and 2

Step 1

this as shown in the photo and use it as a template for cutting the 2x2 side-wall frame pieces F, G, H, and J. Here's how to create two identical side-wall pieces from one sheet of plywood:

- On one edge, measure up and mark at 18 inches.
- On the opposite edge, measure up and mark at 5½ inches.
- Draw a straight line connecting the two marks.
- Cut along this line.

2. Use a sliding T bevel on the plywood to record the angle for cuts on the side-wall frame pieces. The angle will be approximately 26 degrees.

3. Transfer the angle onto pieces F, G, and H. Position one edge of the T bevel against piece F and mark a line from the top outer corner along the angle set by the T bevel. Repeat this step on pieces G and H. Cut all pieces along these lines.

4. Set the side-wall frame pieces onto the plywood to check the fit. Then use 3-inch wood screws to fasten pieces F, G, H, and J together. Note: predrill and/or counter-sink long screws to prevent splitting 2x2 framing. Secure the plywood sheathing to each frame with 1¾-inch screws.

5. Join pieces K and L to form a rectangle. Cut the 57-inch by 18-inch plywood sheathing and secure it to the back wall frame with 1¾-inch screws.

6. Line up the four walls on the raised bed as shown (see next page). Attach walls to each other with 3-inch screws.

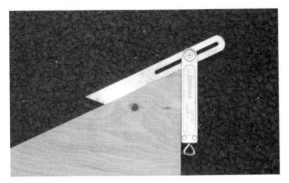

Step 2

Step 4

Step 3

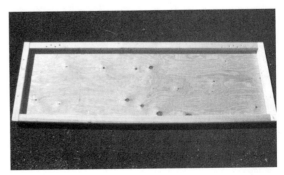

Step 5

Step 6

Step 7

Step 8

7. Assemble the lid frame pieces M, N, and O with 3-inch screws, toenailing the pieces as shown.

8. Flip the lid over and position on top of the back wall of the cold frame.

- Attach 6-inch L brackets at the corners for extra strength, positioning them as shown so the lid sits flush with the box.

- Attach hinges to the cold frame lid 5 inches in from each end with 1¾-inch screws. Mark position of hinge holes on back wall sheathing. Drill ⁵⁄₁₆-inch holes. Insert 2½-inch bolts, add interior washers, and secure with wingnuts.

- Add handle centered on front edge of lid, attached with bolts.

Step 9

9. Attach the cover material to the lid frame with 1-inch washered screws.

10. Use 28-inch-long, 1-inch square hardwood stock as lid stays to vent or hold lid open.

   • Drill $5/16$-inch holes on the square stock, 1 inch from each end.

   • Drill $5/16$-inch holes through each end of raised bed, $3\frac{1}{4}$ inches in from back and 2 inches down from cap. Attach lid stay to raised bed with 3-inch bolt, using flat washers and double nut.

   • Drill $5/16$-inch holes, 3 inches deep, on cold frame lid, $7\frac{1}{2}$ inches and $26\frac{1}{2}$ inches in from front on each end of lid frame.

   • To vent cold frame, lift lid and pivot lid stay to line up with front hole on lid and insert eye bolt.

   • To secure lid all the way open, pivot lid stays to line up with back hole on lid and insert eye bolt.

Completed combined raised bed and cold frame

HOOP-HOUSE CLOCHE

A hoop-house cloche can be sized to fit many garden beds. This design creates a cloche that is $3\frac{1}{2}$ feet wide by 5 feet long and has a center height of approximately 30 inches. Use the chart and details in chapter 8 to adjust these directions to build a cloche to fit your bed dimensions.

Completed hoop-house cloche

Materials

• 9-gauge wire, 48 feet (If bulk wire is not available, source hoops from commercial vendors or create from other materials; see Chapter 8.)

• 4- or 6-mil clear plastic sheeting, at least 8 feet by 10 feet, cut to fit

• 5-foot bamboo or other crosspiece

• Bamboo or other stakes, as needed

• 1x2 lumber, in quantity (see Cutting Instructions)

• Wood lath, in quantity (see Cutting Instructions)

• 1-inch wood screws, in quantity

• Twine

Cutting Instructions

• Wire hoops: 6 @ 8 feet

• 1x2 lumber: 2 @ 60 inches, 4 @ 20 inches

• Wood lath: 4 @ 30 inches, 4 @ 20 inches

Step 4

Steps 1 through 3

Steps 5 and 6

Building and Operating Instructions

1. Position the hoops along one long edge of the bed, 12 inches apart. Two stakes and a string line set up along the edge of the bed help create a nice, straight row. If possible, do not walk on garden bed when installing.

2. Sink ends of each hoop into the soil along the bed edges, 6–12 inches deep.

3. Sink a stake halfway into the ground at the base of each hoop and tether the hoops to the stakes with twine. Note: this step is optional; it may not be necessary unless your garden experiences high winds.

4. Position the crosspiece under the hoops at their highest point and tie it to each hoop with twine. Note: the crosspiece can be bamboo, a commercially sold garden stake, or other material of your choice. Be sure it has no sharp edges or ends, as these could rub and rip the plastic in gusty winds. Cover ends with duct tape if necessary.

5. Roll out enough plastic sheathing to cover the hoops and extend flat on the ground on all sides, at least 6 inches all around.

6. Mark excess plastic, pull the sheet off the hoops and lay it flat to cut off excess, then put the plastic cover back onto the hoops.

Step 7

Step 9

7. Position the long 1x2 lumber against the hoops under the edge of the plastic. Place a long lath piece on top of each one, sandwiching the plastic between them. Screw the lath down every 12 inches to secure the plastic.

8. Repeat with the shorter 1x2 lumber and shorter lath pieces on each end, gathering the plastic as necessary when sandwiching it together to create solid ground-contact on all sides.

9. To access the bed, lift the boards on one side and flip the plastic over the top of the cloche. Note: in high-wind areas, additional hold-downs such as bricks or garden staples may be needed to keep the plastic in place.

SEED-STARTING SHELVES

A thrift-store bookcase or utility-room shelving can be converted into a great seed-starting station. Look for a bookshelf that is 2–3 feet wide by 4–6 feet tall with some movable shelves. Metal utility-room shelving units are good because some are lighter weight or even on wheels. Get one with an open back for good air circulation.

The shelves should be 10–14 inches deep. Each shelf can easily hold a standard seed flat, which measures 21 inches long by 11 inches deep. One flat can be lit by a 21- to 24-inch fluorescent lighting fixture, suspended from the underside of the shelf above. A fixture with two lights is 7 inches deep. The light hangs from a chain so you can move it up as the plants grow.

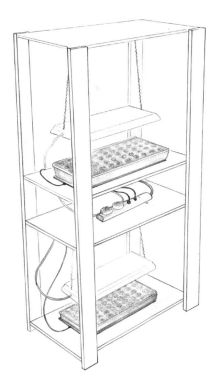

Materials

- Bookcase or shelving unit
- Seed-starting heat mat, 1 per tray
- Seed flat with undertray, cell tray, clear lid
- Seed-starting soil mixture
- Fluorescent lighting fixtures, 21- or 24-inch, with standard bulbs (good) or full-spectrum bulbs (better), 1 per tray
- Small-gauge linked chain, cut to 2-foot sections, 2 per tray
- Small cup hooks or S hooks, sized to accept the links of the chain, 2 per shelf
- Small clamp-on fan, 1 per shelf
- Extension cords, power strip, timer, 1 each per shelf

Building and Operating Instructions

1. Attach two pieces of chain to each light fixture, one on each end.
2. Screw hooks into underside of shelf, centered front to back and about 6 inches from each end. (If your shelving unit has metal-grid shelves, drill holes to hold S hooks from underside of shelf instead.)
3. Place one heat mat and thermostat on shelf, with seed flat assemblage on top of it.
4. Hang grow lights by their chains, level and 2–3 inches above seed tray.

5. Clamp fan onto side wall of shelf, level with top of seed tray and plug heat mat, light, and fan into power strip.
6. If heat mat has a thermostat, set it to recommended temperature.
7. Fill seed trays with damp seed-starter mix and sow seeds. Mark cells clearly with variety names.
8. Keep seed trays consistently damp for germination (clear lid helps).
9. After seedlings emerge, turn off heat mat and turn on grow light. Set timer for twelve to fourteen hours a day.
10. Monitor seedling growth and water needs regularly. The clear lid is optional, but should be removed if plants show signs of damping off disease (see chapter 10). Turn on fan intermittently to strengthen seedlings and prevent damping off, especially after watering. Remove lid when tallest seedlings touch it.

Steps 3 and 4

Completed seed-starting shelves

TRIANGLE TUNNEL

This small tunnel cloche, 48 inches by 18 inches, can be used over one row of plants. It's my own take on a design I first saw built by an Eagle Scout at a community garden in the Portland area. It is assembled with screws, so pieces can be replaced as needed due to rot. The cover is rigid polycarbonate corrugated shed roofing, but six-mil rolled plastic sheathing can be substituted, if desired, and simply stapled onto the frame. Build as many as you need, or enlarge the design to cover multiple rows.

Completed triangle tunnel

Materials

- 2x2 lumber, in quantity (see cutting instructions)
- Plywood, 18 inches x 40 inches
- Clear rigid corrugated plastic sheathing, 26-inch x 8-foot sheet
- 2-inch and 3-inch wood screws, in quantity
- #10 x 1 inch washered screws, in quantity

Cutting Instructions

- Sheathing: (A) 2 plywood triangles with 18-inch base, 20-inch sides; (B) 2 plastic sheets @ 20 x 48 inches
- 2x2 Frame: (C) 2 @13½ inches; (D) 2 @ 16¾ inches; (E) 2 @ 13¼ inches; (F) 2 @ 46 inches; (G) 2 @ 6 inches (handles); (H) 2 @ 14 inches (props)

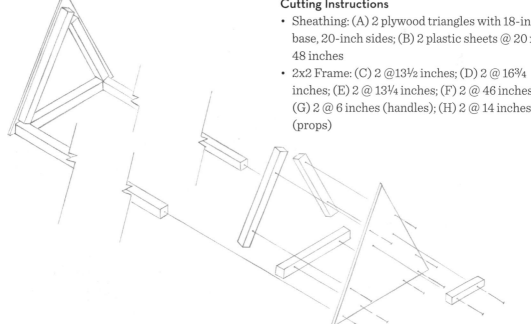

Steps 1 and 2

Step 3

Steps 4 through 6

Building and Operating Instructions

1. Using short screws, attach one base frame C piece to each plywood end, centered.
2. Using short screws, attach D and E to plywood as shown, with bottom corner of each touching base frame C.
3. Stand up plywood ends and, using long screws, attach long F pieces to finish the frame.
4. Using washered screws, attach plastic sheeting. Predrill screw holes in plastic ⅛ inch to 3/16 inch larger than the fastener to allow for natural expansion and contraction of panels. Do not overtighten. Note: the plastic sheathing meets at the top of the triangle but is not fastened. Adjust panels so that one rib of the corrugated plastic overlaps the other. The bottom edge of the plastic should be a half inch above the ground level, and it should overlap the plywood by ½ inch on each end.
5. Using long screws, attach handles G to each plywood end. Predrill holes through handles.
6. Use props H on each end to vent the tunnel as needed. They can be set under one edge or used vertically against the handles.

THREE POPULAR TRELLISES

Trellising warm-season crops can provide more space for cool-season crops, effectively increasing your garden space without adding more land. Here are three easy trellis designs.

A-FRAME

This simple square of mesh-covered wood gets propped up in the bed to support climbing peas, beans, or cucumbers. You can also plant a quick-growing cool-season crop such as salad greens in its shelter before the main crop covers it. Use vinyl-coated wire mesh (mesh with 2-inch by 2½-inch squares is my favorite), or string twine vertically along the frame. Frame dimensions can be modified to fit your garden bed.

Materials

- 1x2 and 2x2 lumber, in quantity (see cutting instructions)
- Wood lath, in quantity
- 1-inch wood screws, 8
- 3-inch wood screws, 4
- ¼-inch x 3-inch bolts, with washers and wingnuts
- Welded-wire mesh or hardware cloth
- Staples

Cutting Instructions

- 2x2 frame: 2 @ 34 inches, 2 @ 48 inches
- 1x2 supports: 2 @ 48 inches
- Lath brackets, 4 @ 19 inches
- Cover material: 36 x 42½ inches

Building and Operating Instructions

1. Using long screws, build the rectangular frame of 2x2 lumber. Predrilling and/or countersinking will prevent splitting of the lumber. Place the crosspieces 2 inches from the ends of the vertical uprights.
2. Using short screws, add a bracket of wood lath at an angle on each corner for strength.

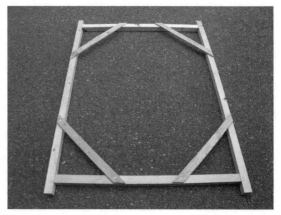

Steps 1 and 2

Completed A-frame trellis

3. Drill a hole three-quarters of an inch from one end of the 1x2 supports and the same distance from the top corners of the frame. Attach supports to frame with bolts and wingnuts. When the trellis is erected, the supports swivel out to create the A shape.

4. Attach welded-wire mesh to the square with staples.

5. Position the A-frame over the bed and plant your vining crop near the mesh edge.

BAMBOO TEPEE

The tepee is the simplest trellis to build, as it requires only a few long poles of bamboo (or other long stakes), a few short stakes, and some twine. Plant runner or pole beans at the base of each pole. These can shelter cool-season salad greens or late-summer brassica seedlings in the center of the bed.

Step 3

Completed bamboo tepee

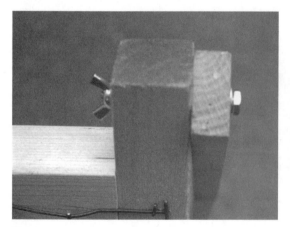

Step 4

Materials

- Bamboo, 3 or more culms (stems)
- Stakes, 12 inches long, in quantity
- Twine

Building and Operating Instructions

1. Lay at least three pieces of dried bamboo culms side by side, with their bottom ends together.
2. About a foot from the top of the shortest bamboo pole, tie all the poles together loosely with a piece of twine, then weave a long end of the twine between them in a figure-eight pattern to securely bind the poles together.
3. Stand the poles on end, spread the trellis upright over the bed, and position the pole ends evenly around the perimeter.
4. Drive stakes into the soil next to each upright trellis pole, and tie each pole to its stake with twine.
5. To increase the growing space, weave twine horizontally between the poles to create a grid pattern, or tie additional lengths of twine at the top before setting up the trellis and bring these down to the ground between the poles.

Step 2

Step 4

Completed welded-wire tunnel

Steps 3 and 4

WELDED-WIRE TUNNEL

Welded-wire grid fencing can be put to good use for growing lightweight vining crops and, as with the A-frame, you can plant a short-season cool crop under it while the main crop is growing. In addition to or instead of the fencing, the tunnel can be covered with plastic sheathing to make a cloche or with floating row cover to make a shade house. The fencing usually comes in rolls of 24- to 48-inch heights, vinyl coated or galvanized. The hoops and mesh can be tied together with vinyl zip-ties, but I like to use inexpensive twine, which can be cut away with a utility knife for quick disassembly.

This design makes a 36-inch-wide tunnel that is 3 feet long. Hoop and mesh lengths can be adjusted to fit your garden bed, but the black poly hoops are not strong enough to support a much wider tunnel.

Materials

- Welded-wire mesh, 36 inches wide, 7 feet long
- Black polyurethane cloche hoops, 3 @ 7 feet
- Bamboo crosspiece, 2 @ 3 feet
- Stakes, 6 @ 18 inches
- Twine

Building and Operating Instructions

1. Lay out stakes along edges of garden bed, 12 inches apart, driven halfway into the soil.
2. Slip the hollow hoop ends over each stake, repeating on each side to make a tunnel.
3. Using twine, tie the crosspieces onto the hoops two-thirds of the way up each side of the tunnel.
4. Using twine, attach the welded-wire mesh to the hoops.

Resources

In the past, season-extension materials and green-house supplies such as twin-wall polycarbonate could be purchased only by mail-order. Today, more and more plant nurseries and hardware stores offer some of these items. Below is a list of mail-order and online sources, but try your local retailers to save shipping costs.

SOURCES FOR SEASON-EXTENSION MATERIALS

A. M. Leonard Co., Piqua, Ohio, www.amleo.com

Charley's Greenhouse and Garden, Mount Vernon, Washington, www.charleysgreenhouse.com

DripWorks, Willits, California, www.dripworks.com

Gardener's Supply Co., Burlington, Vermont, www.gardeners.com

Grower's Supply, a division of FarmTek, Dyersville, Iowa, www.growerssupply.com

Lee Valley Tool Ltd., Ogdensburg, New York, www.leevalley.com

Peaceful Valley Farm and Garden Supply, Grass Valley, California, www.groworganic.com

Books

Ashworth, Suzanne. *Seed to Seed: Seed Saving and Growing Techniques for Vegetable Gardeners.* 2nd ed. Decorah, IA: Seed Savers Publications, 2002.

Bradley, Fern Marshall, and Barbara W. Ellis, eds. *Rodale's All-New Encyclopedia of Organic Gardening.* Emmaus, PA: Rodale Press, 1993.

Brenzel, Kathleen, ed. *Sunset Western Garden Book.* Menlo Park, CA: Sunset Publishing, 2012.

Chalker-Scott, Linda. *The Informed Gardener.* Seattle: University of Washington Press, 2008.

———. *The Informed Gardener Blooms Again.* Seattle: University of Washington Press, 2010.

———. *Sustainable Landscapes and Gardens.* Yakima, WA: GFG Publishing, 2009.

Colebrook, Binda. *Winter Gardening in the Maritime Northwest.* Gabriola Island, BC: New Society Publishers, 2012.

Coleman, Eliot. *Four Season Harvest.* White River Junction, VT: Chelsea Green Publishing, 1999.

Cranshaw, Whitney. *Garden Insects of North America.* Princeton, NJ: Princeton University Press, 2004.

Creasy, Rosalind. *Edible Landscaping.* 2nd ed. San Francisco: Sierra Club Books, 2010.

Deardorff, David, and Kathryn Wadsworth. *What's Wrong With My Plant?* Portland, OR: Timber Press, 2009.

Engeland, Ron. *Growing Great Garlic.* Okanogan, WA: Filaree Productions, 1991.

Gatter, Mark, and Andy McKee. *How to Grow Food in Your Polytunnel.* Devon, England: Green Books, 2010.

Greene, Wesley. *Vegetable Gardening the Colonial Williamsburg Way.* New York: Rodale, 2012.

Head, William. *Gardening Under Cover: A Northwest Guide to Solar Greenhouses, Cold Frames, and Cloches.* Seattle: Sasquatch Books, 1989. (Out of print.)

Jeavons, John. *How to Grow More Vegetables (than you ever thought possible on less land than you can imagine).* 7th ed. Berkeley, CA: Ten Speed Press, 2006.

Link, Russell. *Landscaping for Wildlife in the Pacific Northwest.* Seattle: University of Washington Press, 1999.

Mass, Cliff. *The Weather of the Pacific Northwest.* Seattle: University of Washington Press, 2008.

Seattle Tilth Association. *The Maritime Northwest Gardening Guide.* Rev. ed. Seattle: Seattle Tilth Association, 2007.

Solomon, Steve. *Growing Vegetables West of the Cascades.* 6th ed. Seattle: Sasquatch Books, 2007.

SEED COMPANIES

An asterisk (*) denotes a bioregional company selling seeds adapted to a short-season or maritime climate.

*Abundant Life Seeds, Cottage Grove, Oregon, www.abundantlifeseeds.com

*Fedco Seed Co., Waterville, Maine, www.fedcoseeds.com

Filaree Farm, Okanogan, Washington, www.filareefarm.com

Irish Eyes Garden Seeds, Ellensburg, Washington, www.gardencityseeds.net

*Johnny's Selected Seeds, Winslow, Maine, www.johnnyseeds.com

Kitazawa Seed Co., Oakland, California, www.kitazawaseed.com

Seed Savers Exchange, Decorah, Iowa, www.seedsavers.org

*Territorial Seed Co., Cottage Grove, Oregon, www.territorialseed.com

*Uprising Seeds, Bellingham, Washington, www.uprisingorganics.com

Victory Seed Co., Molalla, Oregon, www.victoryseeds.com

*Wild Garden Seed, Philomath, Oregon, www.wildgardenseed.com

Canadian Seed Companies

Because of customs regulations, some of these companies will ship seeds only to Canada.

Boundary Garlic Farm, Midway, British Columbia, www.garlicfarm.ca

The Cottage Gardener, Newtonville, Ontario, www.cottagegardener.com

*Salt Spring Seeds, Salt Spring Island, British Columbia, www.saltspringseeds.com

Seeds of Victoria, Victoria, British Columbia, http://earthfuture.com/gardenpath

Stellar Seeds, Kaslo, British Columbia, www.stellarseeds.com

West Coast Seeds, Delta, British Columbia, www.westcoastseeds.com

GARDENING AND FOOD-FOCUSED EDUCATIONAL ORGANIZATIONS

Center for Urban Agriculture at Fairview Gardens, Goleta, California, www.fairviewgardens.org

Community Food Security Coalition, Portland, Oregon, www.foodsecurity.org

Earth Island Institute, Berkeley, California, www.earthisland.org

Food Alliance, Portland, Oregon,
www.foodalliance.org

Local Harvest, Santa Cruz, California,
www.localharvest.org

Oregon Tilth, Corvallis, Oregon,
www.tilth.org

Rodale Institute, Kutztown, Pennsylvania,
www.rodaleinstitute.org

Seattle Tilth, Seattle, Washington,
www.seattletilth.org

WEATHER WEBSITES

AgriMet, US Department of Interior, Pacific Northwest
region, www.usbr.gov/pn/agrimet/

Dave's Garden, www.davesgarden.com

KING 5, Seattle, www.king5.com/weather

National Weather Service, www.weather.gov

Oregon Live, Portland, www.oregonlive.com

RainWatch, Seattle, www.atmos.washington.edu/SPU/

Washington State University, www.weather.wsu.edu

Weather Channel, www.weather.com

Weather Network, Canada, www.weathernetwork.com

Weather Underground, www.wunderground.com

Western Regional Climate Center, www.wrcc.dri.edu

Index